BOWLING DOWN THE YEARS

First edition, published in 2000 by

WOODFIELD PUBLISHING
Woodfield House, Babsham Lane, Bognor Regis
West Sussex PO21 5EL, England.

© Frank Eeles, 2000

All rights reserved.
No part of this publication may be reproduced
or transmitted in any form or by any means,
electronic or mechanical, nor may it be stored
in any information storage and retrieval system,
without prior permission from the publisher.

ISBN 1-873203-62-4

Front cover photograph:
'A Bunch of Old Bowlers'
courtesy of **The Rose Studio**

Bowling Down the Years

The history of the Portsmouth & District Bowling Association 1925 - 2000

FRANK EELES

Woodfield Publishing
BOGNOR REGIS • WEST SUSSEX • ENGLAND

*To my Father who introduced me to bowls,
and to my wife who has been a
great help in researching this book.*

An old photograph from the archives of Portsmouth City Records Office.

Foreword

I felt that to record the history of the Portsmouth & District Bowling Association (originally called Portsmouth & District Bowling Leagues), in their 75th year, is an attempt to put on paper some historical facts before they disappear into oblivion and into folklore.

It is interesting to note that with forethought and forward vision, eight clubs in the Portsmouth & District area started the Hampshire Bowling Association, which was in the same year that the English Bowling Association was formed, and one can only deduce that the HBA was prompted by the newly formed EBA. Before then it is thought that the type of bowls being played in the area was based very much on the Old English game, as some of the old photographs show.

Most players in the early days were either Aldermen, Councillors, businessmen, and well to do people, and the game was played at a much more leisurely manner than that of today's pace, with much emphasis on the social side of the sport. Ladies seem to have taken a fairly active part in the early days as some old photographs show, and it was not until later that divisions were set up between the sexes, on whose instigation is not quite clear, but in recent years the pendulum has swung back with more mixed clubs being formed.

Over the years it must be noted that bowlers have given quite a lot to charity as you will see from the following pages, with clubs devoting time in their very busy calendar to competitions in aid of local charities. Who says that bowlers are a stingy lot?

In the early days of the Portsmouth & District individual competitions were mainly the responsibility of the Hampshire

County Bowling Association, with the District taking care of the needs of players who wanted to play league bowls.

It is hoped that this publication will spur on younger members of our society to take up the game of bowls, and carry on playing throughout their lives and derive as much enjoyment and pleasure that older players get from the game.

I feel that clubs have a duty to keep accurate records of their club's activities and achievements, so that future generations may look back with some accuracy as to what was going on in our game. In this respect honours boards, which as we know take up a lot of wall space in the clubhouse, can be professionally photographed and framed, and the boards used again for current use. With the advent of the computer and the digital camera, records can easily be stored on databases.

The records produced in this book are as accurate as the information received and researched, and every endeavour has been made to avoid errors, however if anyone has proof of any inaccuracies would they please let the writer know.

This book has been produced with the help of a 'Millennium Festival Awards for All' grant.

I trust that you find this book of interest.

Frank Eeles.

Contents

Foreword 5
The Hampshire Bowling Association 9
Before 1903 11
1896 • Southsea Waverley BC 14
1902 • City of Portsmouth 17
1914 • Copnor 20
1914 • Star & Crescent 22
1921 • Alexandra B&SC 24
1923 • Milton Park BC 27
1923 • Pembroke Gardens BC 30
1923 • Portsmouth Civil Service BC 31
1925 • Gosport BC 33
1926 • Priory BC 36
1932 • College Park BC 38
1933 • Waterlooville BC 40
1934 • Co-operative BC 42
1934 • Cosham BC 43
1938 • Forton BC 45
1939-45 • The War Years 47
1947 • Eastney B.C. 50
1948 • Lakeside BC 51
1949 • Highbury BC 53
1950 • Gas Social B.C. 55
1961 • Bridgemary B.C. 56
1963 • Naismith B.C. 57
1965 • Leigh Park BC 58
1969 • Portsmouth Water Company B.C. 60
1970 • Rowner B.C. 62
1972 • IBM Bowls Club 63
1974 • Fareham BC 65
1976 • Vosper Thornycroft BC 67
1977 • Hayling Island BC 68
1979 • Lee on the Solent 70
1980 • Crofton BC 73

BOWLING DOWN THE YEARS · **7**

1982 • Purbrook Heath BC	75
1984 • Bedhampton BC	77
1985 • Portsmouth Post Office BC	79
1986 • Drayton Park	81
1986 • Portchester BC	83
1989 • Cowplain BC	85
1990 • Denmead BC	86
1994 • Southsea Falcon BC	89
1996 • Emsworth BC	91
The Queens BC, Gosport	93
EBA Presidents	97
International Players	97
EBA National Competitions	97
Hampshire County BA Presidents	99
Hampshire County Competitions	101
P&D Presidents 1925 – 1959	110
P&D Presidents 1960 – 1993	111
P&D Presidents 1994 – 2000	112
Keith Cross	113
League Championships	116
League Champions	120
Trophies for Combination Leagues	128
Trophies for Competitions	129
The Leagues, Past, Present, and Future	129
The Gwyn Guy Trophy	131
The Rowland Cup	133
The Mayors Charities Bowling Shield	136
The Southsea Open Tournament	137
Bowling Greens	139
The Future	141
Club Names from The Past	142
Acknowledgements	143
Commandments of Bowling	144

The Hampshire Bowling Association

This Association was founded on the 9th February 1903 with eight bowling clubs from the Portsmouth and Gosport area. This coincided in the same year that the English Bowling Association was founded, and was 17 years prior to the present Hampshire County Bowling Association. Records show that the following clubs were involved.

Alverstoke BC – Still playing and now known as Alverstoke Old English BC

Carisbrooke BC – Little known of this club but could be a name of a hotel, road, or even from the Isle of Wight.

North End BC – Played originally in Kingston Crescent and were known as Kingston Cross BC Still in being and playing Old English

Portsmouth BC – Later known as Portsmouth Corporation, now City of Portsmouth.

Queens BC – Green built on, but the club is still there in Queens Road.

Saxe-Weimar BC – Now known as Southsea Waverley.

Southsea BC – Now known as Southsea Falcon.

Victoria BC – This was situated behind the Pelham Hotel in Chichester Road, and became one of the most popular clubs in the County, but sadly no more.

A Challenge Shield Trophy which was presented by Portsmouth BC was competed for and the first winners in 1903 were Saxe-Weimar BC.

A second shield was presented to the Association by Saxe-Weimar BC, and in this instance the first winners were Queens BC.

A singles competition was introduced in 1904. The first winner was W.C. Bower (Carisbrooke), and was presented with a Gold Medal donated by Major J.E. Pink, JP.

Records do not show when this Association disbanded, but it is thought that this could have been at the outbreak of World War One.

One of the original shields presented to the Hampshire Bowling Association in 1903.

Before 1903*

Could it be that Adam and Eve rolled apples along the ground in the Garden of Eden to amuse themselves?

Could it be that prehistoric man picked up a round stone and trundled it to some object for fun?

We know that the allied game of skittles became first known in 5200 BC. The Chinese, at that time, trundled stones towards a hole in the ground to as near the lip as possible; if it fell in it did not count. There is a picture of bowls in Egypt about 3000 BC and in fact in almost every part of the world a bowls-like game was played in very early times.

Could it be that the French started the game from Roman influence and brought it over in 1066?

We know that a bowling green is mentioned in the records of Chichester Castle soon after 1066.

Could it be that a game called 'Jacto Lapidium' was the origin of 'Jack' and that our term bowls came from the Latin 'bulla' used for ball games in general?

We know that the earliest known drawing of bowls is 13th Century and is in the library of Windsor Castle.

We know that despite facing many difficulties at times, there exist many pictures of bowls being played in the 16th, 17th and 18th Centuries.

Could it be that the most famous of these, that of Drake on Plymouth Hoe was fact or fiction?

---

*_We know that_ = FACT   _Could it be that_ = CONJECTURE

BOWLING DOWN THE YEARS · 11

We know that in those times greens were hand scythed rough grass, varied in length, full of bumps and were without ditches.

We know that the Southampton site was in use prior to 1299; Christchurch claiming 1100; Bedford Priory about 1220 and Halesworth Angel (Suffolk) over 500 years old; and that there are many clubs able to trace their history back well over 200 years.

We know that in Tewkesbury in 1469 a great concourse of people assembled at the bowling green.

We know that bowls was prohibited by the King as interfering with archery and in 1477 anyone caught in the act was liable to two years in prison and a fine of £10.

We know that Henry VIII had his own green at Hampton Court and there are records of his losses from £4 to £35, so in 1541 the profit motive was removed and no one could establish a green for gain – this was in force until 1845.

We know that our game is mentioned in Shakespeare's plays. Charles I had a green laid for him when he was a prisoner in Carisbrooke Castle. Charles II was a great bowler and was able to play on a much improved surface by the planting of camomile, which was frequently scythed; along with the Duke of York and the Duke of Buckingham he drew up a set of rules in 1670, containing a number of similarities to those in force today – one rule was 'always keep your temper'.

We know that in 1848 a meeting took place in Glasgow Town Hall and that some 200 representatives attended and that William Mitchell, a Glasgow Solicitor, produced a set of rules which were adopted and came into general use.

We know that in 1888 there were 364 clubs in Scotland and in 1892 the Scottish Bowling Association was formed.

We know that this enthusiasm overflowed into England, the Municipal Corporation Act of 1835 helped to get public gardens and games facilities and the Local Government Act – 1888 (the foundation of our local government system) gave much impetus.

We know that in 1899, bowlers who were also interested in England v Australia cricket questioned as to why this could not be applied to bowls, a man named S. Yelland set to work on the problem and as a result the Imperial Bowling Association was formed primarily to arrange games against Australia, Dr. W. G. Grace became interested, being on the verge of retirement from cricket, and in 1901 he led an English team against Scotland and learned about the Scottish Association.

We know that the Imperial Bowling Association was asked to have a member on the committee to assist with the formation of the English Bowling Association, but it was not done for some time.

This extract is from the book History of the E.B.A. which is currently being collated to celebrate their centenary in 2003 and is reproduced by kind permission of Fred J. Inch, Deputy Secretary E.B.A.

1896 • Southsea Waverley BC

The club was formed in 1896, played on the green situated in Saxe-Weimar Road, Southsea and adopted their name from the road in which it was situated. Saxe-Weimar Road was changed to Waverley Road at the outbreak of World War 1, when German names were not favoured and the club therefore changed its name to Southsea Waverley BC.

In 1903, Saxe-Weimar was one of eight local bowling clubs which formed the Hampshire Bowling Association; this coincided with the formation of the English Bowling Association and was 17 years prior to the official formation of the Hampshire County Bowling Association.

Saxe-Weimar were the first winners of the "Challenge Shield Trophy" which was presented to the Hampshire BA by G.W. Corbin, a Town Councillor and member of Portsmouth Bowling Club.

In 1907 it was reported in the official Southsea & Portsmouth guide that the club had 'over 200 members' and that 'trams pass the door'; it also states that for the sum of 2/6d (12.5p) per month, visitors to the town may become 'Temporary Members'. The club at that time had two billiard tables and among the members were some fine cueists. It was also reported that the green had been recently relaid with Down Turf, and the guide states "the bowling green is a first class one, no expense having been spared to make it perfect". Early photographs show that to the west of the green the skyline is dominated by a windmill called Dock Mill, which was in Napier Road. It was demolished in 1923.

In 1924 the club purchased the house on the west side of the green and extended the clubhouse to include the house. The official opening ceremony on the 30th October 1924 was performed by the Mayor of Portsmouth, Alderman G.W.

Corbin, in the presence of the President H. Marchment, and members.

The club has a fine record in providing members as Officers to the highest level in the bowling world, notably was the appointment in 1969 when J.S. Mill became the President of the English Bowling Association. The club has provided the following County Presidents, namely: 1952 W. Christopher, 1956 J.S. Mill, 1964 E.A. Rogers, 1976 A.R. Bendall, and in 1984 C.E. Petch.

Portsmouth & District Presidents have been: 1927 W.H. Knight, 1932 E. Ridsdale, 1948 W. Chistopher, 1950 J.S. Mill, 1960 C.E. Petch, 1968 J.H. Lubin, 1969 A. Bendall, 1979 G.H. Loosley, and 1983 J. A. Whitehill.

Many individual honours have come to Southsea Waverley. In 1933 B. Matthews, H. Head, H. Johnson, and J. Rhodes (skip) won the EBA Fours Championship, and in 1986 a rink skipped by Dusty Miller won the EBA Top Fours Competition.

Southsea Waverley/Saxe-Weimar club house circa 1908, with Dock Mill in the background.

Saxe-Weimar bowlers: first winners of the Hampshire Bowling Association, 'Challenge Sheild' in 1903.

Over the years Hampshire County titles have been won by Waverley players. The County Pairs title has been won by W. Knight and W. Lenton in 1926, J. Rhodes and H. Johnson in 1933 and A. Bendall and T. Emmerson in 1972. The County Triples title has been won by Waverley players in 1952, 1959, and 1964. The County Fours title in 1933 and the 2 Wood Triples title in 1971.

Many Portsmouth and District titles have been won over the years. Team effort seems to be the clubs forte, having won the League Division 1 title on 10 occasions, and in the runners up spot 16 times. The club have won the County Cup three times. In 1929, 1953 and 1981.

In keeping with the club's early members who had forward thinking, the Southsea Waverley now boast an active golf society and play on a regular basis.

1902 • City of Portsmouth

The club was inaugurated in 1901, and the Bowling Green which was sited at the North End Recreation Ground, was opened for play in June 1902 by the then Mayor, Sir W. T. Dupree, JP The club used the title of Portsmouth Corporation Bowling Club. These were the first public greens in Portsmouth, To get to the Recreation Ground in those days one took a number 1d tram from the Town Hall getting off at North End and walking through Gladys Avenue, described as a five minute walk.

There was a very strong representation of Councillors with at least nine being Patrons of the club, including the Mayor of Portsmouth. From information received a club was formed by Portsmouth Councillors Sir H. Pink and J. Pink (Grocers), Sir W.T. Dupree (Brickwoods Brewery), J. Timpson and T. Rowland. It was called North End Bowls Club, and was situated in Stubbington Avenue. These gentlemen were some of the original Patrons of Portsmouth Corporation Bowling Club.

The membership in 1902 was 30. The first President was Councillor Charles Gillett, JP, followed by Councillor S.E. Spriggins (1903-1906), and then Councillor J. Timpson (1907-1913). By 1913 the membership had increased to 200.

The green in those days was described as "being in flourishing condition, due to the preparation by the groundsman H. Edmunds".

The clubs headquarters were at the Avenue Hotel in Twyford Avenue, where they held their meetings. The clubs first Secretary was Mr. Hales, who had a Newsagents shop in Twyford Avenue.

Sometime before 1921 J. Timpson, H. Edmunds and other members of the club decided to purchase some land nearby

City of Portsmouth Corporation Bowling Green, North End Recreation Ground (now Alexandra Park).

Bowling Tournament at North End Recreation Ground, early 1900's.

to form a private club, and continued to play as the Portsmouth Corporation until the new green and clubhouse was available for play.

The new green was opened for the start of the 1921 season. Records show that the club transferred over to the new green, and later that year changed their name to Alexandra Bowling & Social Club. Obviously not all members transferred and they continued to play on the North End Recreation Ground.

It is not clear what happened during the interim period but in 1926 the clubs name was changed to City of Portsmouth, and at the same time the North End Recreation Ground was renamed Alexandra Park.

D. Harvey won the Hampshire County singles title in 1933. The club has had a chequered history over its long existence. Some of the highlights were winning the Rowland Cup in 1932, 1948 and 1959. League honours include winning Division 1 in 1927 and 1931, Division 2 in 1951, 1954, & 1976. Division 3 in 1974, and Division 4 in 1994.

During the Second World War 1939-1945 one green was kept open, so consequently activities at the club have been non-stop since 1902.

The club can boast that they have had the honour of proposing four Presidents for the Portsmouth & District B. A. In 1935 J. Williams, 1938 H. Brewer, 1943 H. Brewer, and 1999 B. Ivemey.

1914 • *Copnor*

Although the club was not formed until 1914, it is reported that the green was constructed in 1908. The name Sawyer is strongly represented in the history of Copnor BC. George Frederick Sawyer lived opposite the green in Tangier Road, and shortly after World War 1 became the Secretary of the club until 1954, at which time his son Harold took over the Secretary's job, and held that position until 1997, some 79 years in the Sawyer family.

Harold clearly remembers as a small lad watching his father from an upstairs window of their house, bowling on the green. This obviously stood him in good stead for later years, and started his serious bowling at the age of sixteen. This eventually resulted in International honours coming his way in 1974 when he represented England against Scotland, Ireland, and Wales in Edinburgh. Harold has also represented the County on 106 occasions in the Middleton Cup competition, and was in the winning Hampshire teams in1963 against Essex, 1967 against Middlesex, 1968 against Suffolk, and again 1971 against Middlesex. In his first Middleton Cup Final, Harold was in a rink skipped by J. Fairburn that won 37 shots to 6.

The club has had its fair share of honours over the years notably winning the County Club Championship in 1956. The club was Division 1 titleholders in 1942 and Division 2 winners in 1965, 1978, 1983, & 1992. They won the Rowland Cup in 1936, 1946, 1967 and 1975. The club also won the Mayors Charity Shield in 1937 and 1952.

E.C. Smith of the Copnor BC became President of the Portsmouth and District BA in 1956.

Individual titles have also come to Copnor in recent years, notably in 1975 when J. Beveridge, R. Gaiger & S. Wild won the Hampshire County 2 wood triples title, and in 1998 when the three Dave's, Grant, Kingswell, and Powe won the District Triples title.

The Hampshire County Hon. Secretaries Singles title has been won on no fewer than eight occasions by a Copnor Secretary, and there are no prizes for guessing who that Secretary was, but to give you a clue his initials are H. S. These titles were won between 1956 and 1975.

Copnor BC remains a small, friendly, yet very competitive club, and are part of the Copnor Bridge Bowling Association, who lease the green from the Portsmouth City Council.

Harold Sawyer, England International, 1974.

1914 • *Star & Crescent*

On March 7th 1914 a group of eight bowlers met in the home of Councillor E.S. Main at 79 Festing Grove, Southsea to discuss the possibility of forming a bowling club in the Canoe Lake area of Southsea. A public meeting was held shortly afterwards in the Festing Hotel. The hotel's proprietor, Councillor Main, was duly elected as the club's first President. The Portsmouth Council Superintendent of Parks, Mr H. Edmunds, gave the necessary approval. The Council's annual fee was 2/6d and membership of the club initially was 5/-.

The Mayor of Portsmouth, Alderman J.H. Corke, JP officially opened the club in May 1914, and the club's first match was on the 9th May 1914. Due to all the assistance given to the club by the Portsmouth Council Alderman J.H. Corke was asked to become the club's Patron; at the same time, three Aldermen and eleven Councillors were made Vice Presidents. With all the help given by the Council in getting the club running, it was decided to adopt the Portsmouth Coat of Arms as their badge and the name Star & Crescent was taken.

From early club records in 1914 the Committee were discussing the restriction of non-biased woods. (This could be similar to discussions in more recent years with the introduction of narrow running bowls currently being produced). A Ladies section was formed in 1914. In July 1915, records show that of the first member being "thrown out".

In September 1920 the first match played under EBA rules was played on the green; up until this time only four recognised clubs were using biased woods in the Portsmouth area. The club became affiliated to the Hampshire County BA in 1922 and in 1925 together with seven other local clubs became Founder members of the Portsmouth & District BA.

In 1926 the green was out of use for reasons which are not too clear. The club had to play its matches on other greens and it is understood that the Council had to spend £200 to bring the green up to EBA standards.

By 1933 the cost of a season ticket had risen to 21 shillings. In 1939 the club appointed W.H. Griffin as their first Life President. The green was closed in 1940 due to the Second World War as was not reopened until the 1945 season.

The club's present Pavilion was rebuilt at a cost of £5,000 and was opened in 1965 by the Mayor of Portsmouth, Alderman Frank Lines.

The club has had its fair share of successes by winning the league Division 1 title on eight occasions: 1967, 1968, 1970, 1973, 1974, 1975, 1979 and 1981. The Division 2 title has been won four times: 1938, 1953, 1994 and 1996. The club has won the Rowland Cup in 1980 and 1998, and were also winners of the Mayors Charity Shield in 1933, 1934, 1936, 1954 and 1956. The pinnacle came in 1973 when the club won the County Club Championship.

Individual members have accounted for some Hampshire County titles. In 1959 A. Randal won the singles title. The pairs title was won in 1967 by C. Watts and R. Lillington and again in 1980 by E. Brown and K. Grout. The County triples title in has been won in 1963 and 1983.

Many P&D titles have been won by members, notably the Champion of Champions title in 1973 by R. Dickie.

The following members have been Portsmouth & District BA Presidents: 1930 W. Griffin; 1939 & 1940 J. England; 1946 E. Allen; 1972 J. Sorrell; 1973 H. Moody; 1986 R. Edmonds; 1988 Capt. D. Bateman and more recently in 1998, S. Sprake. It is notable that in 1966 C. Watts was appointed as club Secretary, a position he was to hold for 22 years.

1921 • *Alexandra B&SC*

Sometime before 1921, some members of the Portsmouth Corporation BC who played on the North End Recreation Ground decided to purchase some land nearby to build a private bowling green and premises. The cost of the land was £620. The money was raised by debentures, which paid 6% per annum. It is recorded that by May 1921 the land had been fully paid for.

The new green opened for the 1921 season. The first President was J. Timpson and the first Captain was H. Edmunds. The membership was around 130. The club started life as the Portsmouth Corporation Bowls Club, but on the 8th June 1921 at a club meeting the name was changed to Alexandra Bowling & Social Club.

The opening of the club premises was performed on the 20th July 1921. The programme of events was to be a Ladies Bowling match, followed by the official opening by the Mayor of Portsmouth, and light refreshments. The City's Tramway Band was asked to play in the interval.

The club affiliated to the EBA in 1923. In 1924 the club received a circular from the Portsmouth & District Bowling Leagues outlining the league rules, and 4 delegates were appointed to represent the club at the League Rules meeting. Later that year the club entered two teams in the leagues and therefore became one of the founder members of the P&D.

In 1927 J. Rose became the President of the Portsmouth & District Bowling Leagues, and in 1930 he became the Hampshire County Bowling Association President.

The club entered the County Club Championship for the first time in 1928, and in the first round played the City of Portsmouth.

In 1930 discussion was taking place in committee on the possibility of building an Indoor Bowling Hall. Much discussion took place over the next few years but no decision was reached.

In the early days the club was very socially orientated, with various activities besides Bowling such as Tennis, Whist Drives, Concerts, Dances, Children's Parties, Snooker and Billiards, and Charabanc Outings. Such was the activity of the card players that the club was getting through six packs of cards per month, which resulted in a levy of one penny per month being made to the card players.

More money was raised by debentures so that the club could erect an extension to the original clubhouse. This was

John North bowling first bowl of season in his Hampshire County Presidential year, 1980.

opened by the President Lt. Cdr. W.J. Pavey, RN in 1936. A Plaque was erected on the outside of the building to mark the occasion.

During the war years the club offered the use of their green and facilities to other clubs in the area who had lost the use of their own greens to the military. Due to the probable lack of warehouse space in the City for removal and storage operators, part of the clubhouse was rented out, and for the most part contained furniture being stored.

J.B. North was President of the P&D in 1975, and in 1980 became the President of the Hampshire County Bowling Association. Other Presidents of the P&D were 1926 J. E. Rose, 1931 F.W. Neate, 1936 J.A. Goodchild, 1947 W. Hooper, 1957 G.A. Evans, 1985 C. Thompson, and 1991 R. Standley

The club has won many honours over the years for team events some of which are listed here. They have won the League Division 1 title on 10 occasions: 1945, 1971, 1972, 1977, 1978, 1983, 1984, 1985, 1987 & 1988. The Rowland Cup has been won by the club in 1934, 1969, 1981, 1988, 1989 & 1994. The Mayors Charity Shield was won in 1932, and in 1984 won the County Club Championship. Individual honours have also been many in County and District competitions.

The club is one of the keenest supporters of the Portsmouth & District BA, and for many years has hosted the District President's day and the District currently hold their AGM at the Alexandra B&SC.

The clubhouse underwent a major refurbishment in 1994, opened by the Lord Mayor of Portsmouth Councillor Alex Bentley.

1923 • *Milton Park BC*

On February 20th 1923 a well attended meeting of local residents was held at Fishborne Road School for the purpose of forming a bowling club. It was agreed at this meeting that the club should be known as the Milton Park Bowling Club. Councillor J. W. Perkins who was the Chaiman of the Parks Committee on the Portsmouth Council was elected as the clubs first President. Club subscriptions for the year was agreed at 15 shillings.

Although the green was not available until later that year the membership increased and by April 1923 the membership had grown to some 60 bowlers. There was no pavilion and the club asked the Portsmouth Council Parks and Open Spaces Committee for permission to play at Canoe Lake and North End Recreation Ground (Alexandra Park).

On July 11th 1923 the Milton Park green was formally opened, and commenced with a match between the Presidents team and a team representing the Mayor of Portsmouth. It is interesting to note that the cost of entertaining of the guests that day was limited to a total of £6.

In 1923 Taylor Rolph size 3 woods cost 52/- per pair. The Milton Park Annual Dinner cost 5/- per head, and the club Treasurer reported that the club had a surplus of income over expenditure of £13.1.9d for the year. On the 12th December 1923 the first Hon. Secretary's report states "The Club is now a strong going concern and with the hearty co-operation of all the members there is no doubt that it will be, and should be the Premier Bowling Club in the Town".

By 1925 the membership had increased to 102 members, at long last the pavilion was finished and discussions took place regarding a second green.

In 1929, when the new Cumberland turf green had been completed, Milton Park BC moved across to the new green and at the same time the East Anglians BC (Priory) took over the original green that Milton Park had been using.

In the 1930s the Club won the Portsmouth & District League Division 1 title nine times, missing out only in 1931, and in 1936 they won all of their league matches. During the War Years events were organised to raise funds for the Red Cross.

Milton Park can boast that they are one of the most successful clubs in the district as records show...

Hampshire County Club Champions in 1958, and 1963, and runners up on six other occasions.

Portsmouth & District League Division 1 Champions: 1930, 1932, 1933, 1934, 1935, 1936, 1937, 1938, 1939, 1947, 1948, 1950, 1952, 1954, 1956, 1957, 1958, 1961, 1962, 1963, 1964 and 1965.

Rowland Cup Winners: 1929, 1951, 1956, & 1961.

Mayors Charity Shield Winners in 1930 & 1938.

Waverley Shield Winners in 1961.

County Club Championship 1958 & 1963.

Individual County titles have also come Milton Park's way. K. Williams won the County singles title in 1948. The County pairs title was won in 1934 by C. Curtis & E. Phillips and was won again in 1935 by A. Smith & J. Green. The County Triples title was won in 1957 by F. Forward, S. Wyborn & K. Cross.

The County Fours title was won by F. Forward, A. Williams, K. Williams & P. Henley two years running in 1955 and 1956. This title was taken in 1963 F. Forward, F. Moore, G. Hunt &

K. Cross and again in 1964 by D. Moore, R. Scott, E. Holding & D. Grant.

In 1991 Milton Park BC and 3 other Clubs using the two greens at Milton Park formed an Association and jointly pressed ahead with applications for funds to enlarge the pavilion. With the help of a Lottery Sports Fund award and help and support from the Portsmouth City Council the extension and improvements were completed in 1997.

The Association now has a pavilion of which they are justifiably proud and look forward with every confidence to the next millennium.

Milton Park: A good crowd watching some important games circa 1930's.

1923 • Pembroke Gardens BC

Early records are unclear and therefore, unfortunately, founder members names are not known, however the club is one of the earliest formed in the district and celebrated its 75th anniversary in 1998. To mark the occasion the club played a match against a representative side from the Portsmouth & District. The club badge shows Nelson in the centre with laurel leaves surround, two bowls and a jack, with the clubs name above.

The club tasted its first success by winning the Waverley Shield and Rowland Cup in 1928 & 1933 and the Mayor's Charity Shield in 1928 & 1931. It must be assumed that the club entered the first league competition in 1925 but had to wait until 1935 to win the Division 2 title, a success that was repeated in 1969, 1974 & 1984. The club has been Division 2 runner-up on no less than ten occasions over the years.

Individual club players have had their successes over the years, notably in 1954 and 1957 when D. Hishon, P. Batchelor, V. Lake, and A. Barrow won through to the Hampshire County Finals, a feat that was repeated in 1973 by a Pembroke triple who were runners up in the County Triples title and presumably went on to represent Hampshire in the National Finals.

Pembroke club players have also had success in the District competitions, and in 1989, and 1990, B. Dixon won the District Champion of Champions.

The club currently plays in Division 4 but look forward to repeating some of the club's earlier successes.

Over the years Pembroke have had four P&D Presidents: 1951 A.H. Barron; 1962 F.C. Street MBE; 1971 Dr J. Hewat; and 1980 J.R. Barron.

1923 • Portsmouth Civil Service BC

The club was formed in 1923 primarily for civil servants in the area. The first President for the club was Alderman J. F. Lee (Mayor of Gosport), who also became the first President of the Portsmouth & District BA. The club's first Captain was H. Collings, and the Secretary was A.J. Wright. Another founder member was Tom Picton who held the position of club Secretary for 28 years, from 1929-1957.

The club started playing at Southsea, and played there up to 1948, at which time the club moved to the present six rink green at Copnor Road. Vice-Admiral L.V. Morgan officially opened the green on the 15th of May 1948.

As the club was a member of the Civil Service Sports Council the club adopted the standard badge for all members nationwide.

Since being at Copnor Road the club has had an impressive record for winning trophies. They have won the Division 1 league title ten times – in 1949, 1966, 1976, 1980, 1989, 1990, 1993, 1996, 1997 & 1999 and were runners up on a further 8 occasions. On one of their rare drops down to Division 2 they bounced back by winning the title in 1961.

The club's cup record is also impressive: they have won the district Rowland Cup 12 times – in 1945, 1962, 1966, 1968, 1976, 1977, 1978, 1979, 1983, 1987, 1991 and 1996.

The greatest of the club's achievements came in 1995 when they won the County Club Championship by defeating Cove in the final and again in 1999 when they defeated Southampton Sports Centre.

Among the individual honours are J. Stainer (International Trialist), Middleton Cup players include T. Akehurst, J. Stainer

(70 appearances), I. Williams, D. Dennis (85 appearances), C. Hayward, and M. Marchant. Current players who have had Middleton Cup appearances whilst with other clubs are D. Moore, and D. Bishop.

After winning the County Fours title in 1967 I. Williams, M. Roberts, D. Hishon, and J. Stainer went on to represent the County in the EBA National Finals, and just fell at the last hurdle to become runner up for the National Title. Other County Fours Titleholders were in 1954 M. Roberts, H. Cripps, J. Stainer, and E. Akehurst, and on two occasions 1979 and 1983 G. Pratt, K. Newell, H. Downton, and D. Dennis won the title. The County Triples title was won in 1989 by G. Pratt, P. Smith and K. Newell and in 1996 by N. Brimecombe, D. Dennis, and C. Hayward. G. Leeson, and E. Akehurst won the County Pairs title in 1960, and in 1999 this title was won by C. Gardner and W. Taws. To crown the 1999 season C. Hayward won the County Singles title, and M. Marchant won the County Under 25 Singles title. C. Hayward went on to reach the Quarter finals of the National Championships held at Worthing.

Club members have won many Portsmouth & District titles over the years.

D. Dennis was appointed County Coach in 1993 and held that position until 1997. Due to illness he had to relinquish the position, and fellow club member T. Grant took over and currently holds that title.

The club had the honour of proposing three P&D Presidents, in 1934 C.E. Robinson, in 1949 J.H. Ward, MBE and in 1961 George Leeson, and as a mark of respect presented the G. Leeson Cup for the over 60's singles District competition. In 1999, M. Marchant represented England in the U-25 indoor international matches.

1925 • *Gosport BC*

Gosport BC was formed in 1925 and played on the Council Green at Anglesey Gardens. This area was formerly known as Kings Bottom. Most of the land on which the club now stands was reclaimed. Workhouse Lake creek extended almost to Anglesey Road at one time. The green was laid with Cumberland turf and a small pavilion was built.

Among the founder members were Councillor H. S. Masterman and Mr W. Matthews who was still playing in the late 1960s when he was well into his nineties. The first President elected was Councillor H.S. Masterman, the following year the President was Councillor W.G. Mogg. Continuing the council connections, Alderman B.A. Kent became President for the next two years. Another prominent member was Mr J. F. Lee, who was the first mayor of Gosport.

The club had the honour of providing the Hampshire County President on two occasions. In 1927 Mr. J.F. Lee became County President, and in 1948 Dr J.C. Glen had the privilege.

It is clear that in those days it was more a game for 'better off' people who had more leisure time. Fortunately it is a game for people from all walks of life now, who mix and play very amicably together.

Gosport's blazer badge was based on the Borough Seal. The ship depicted represents that of Henry de Bois, Bishop of Winchester, sailing into harbour to shelter from a storm raging outside. The vessel beached on the western shores, and out of thankfulness he named the place "God's Port". This was in the year AD 1140.

A ladies Club was formed in 1928 and shared the green. Facilities were very sparse, there was a small wash hand basin with a cold tap and a gas ring in the corner. The toilets were the public ones in Anglesey Road. The ladies of the club have had their fair share of honours over the years.

As membership increased the Club persuaded the Council to improve facilities, and consequently the pavilion was enlarged with toilets being added. In 1977 a second green was constructed, which was grown from seed.

In 1992 the club was privatised, a lease was prepared and agreed by Club Officers and Gosport Council, whereby the Club became responsible for the maintenance of the interior of the clubhouse and the administration of the greens, the Council being responsible for outside maintenance of the clubhouse and tending to the greens.

F. Sellwood who was President of the Portsmouth & District B.A. in 1954, together with his wife introduced their son Ron Sellwood to bowls at the age of twelve. Ron went on to take several Officers positions at the club, and was a bachelor with no immediate family. When Ron died he left his entire estate, including the family home, to the Gosport Club. This legacy enabled the club in 1992 to almost completely rebuild and enlarge the Clubhouse, and as a fitting tribute named the pavilion "The Sellwood Pavilion". A charity rinks competition is run annually by the club whereby teams compete for the "Ron Sellwood Cup".

The club is a very competitive club and over the years have held their own with the best in the area, having won the Rowland cup on two occasions, winning the Division 2 title on six occasions in 1934, 1964, 1967, 1988, 1990 & 1999 and it is surprising that more honours did not come their way, however individuals within the club have tasted success notably in 1971 with R. Pearse winning the County Secretaries Singles; in 1972 W. Parnham, R. Sellwood & R. Pearse winning the County Two woods triples and, more recently, in 1993

N. O'Donovan, H. Orr & D. Collins winning the County Triples. P&D titles have also been won by members.

Besides F. Sellwood, the club has had two other Presidents of the Portsmouth & District BA – F. Snelling in 1970 and N. Townsend in 1989.

Clubs do need active administrative members, and notably in recent years D. Collins is not only active in the Club but also in District and County matters.

The facilities at Gosport are now some of the best in the area, and having two greens is sought after by touring teams, and for competition finals. The club has hosted the Gwyn Guy Trophy (inter County District) competition, which is held on two greens.

Bill Matthews, one of the founder members of Gosport Bowling Club (taken circa 1969).

1926 • Priory BC

In 1926 the East Anglian Whist Club decided that an outdoor pursuit was healthier and formed a bowls club, playing originally on the Southsea Castle Greens, and called themselves the East Anglian Bowling Club. The members at that time were mainly from East Anglia.

The first President was Mr Sax Friston, and the Secretary was Mr A. Carter. Another notable long serving officer of the club was Dr Montague Way, who had the honour of serving as President of the club from 1935 to 1947.

In 1929 the club decided to move to the green vacated by Milton Park BC when Milton Park BC moved to a new green, which had been laid alongside.

By 1934 most of the members were not East Anglians and in September 1934 changed the name to Priory Bowling Club, adopted from the adjacent Priory Crescent.

The club has had its share of County & District honours winning the County Cup in 1948, and also the Rowland Cup in 1938 and 1950. League records show that the club won Division 1 in 1951, Division 2 in 1947, 1957, 1962, 1966 & 1971, and in 1954 won Division 3.

Two of the most successful Priory bowlers were Mr C. Large and Mr J. Stokes, who won the Hampshire County Bowling Association pairs competition in 1951 and went on to represent the county in the Middleton Cup.

Mention at this point must be made concerning Mr E. Bulbeck who joined the club in 1958, was a past President of the club and on the 17th March 1999 celebrated his 102nd birthday. Two members have served as President of the Portsmouth & District Bowling Association, namely R.W. Balmer in 1974, and E. Facey in 1978.

Much research was carried out by T. Hair and T. Roberts, and later by E. Bulbeck to see whether or not there was any evidence of a Priory nearby, nothing was found and the club adopted their club badge from the Fitzherbert family, who in the middle ages owned most of the land around the area. The club badge is registered as "Three falcons argent with their belles and jesses ore on a sable background, a shield with argent border, scroll with the word Priory"

Bowls is a young man's game, that older people can play
David Bryant CBE

❖ ❖ ❖

Bowlers who say that Leads should stay as Leads,
Are usually Skips who wish to remain as Skips.

❖ ❖ ❖

It is sometimes suggested that the game of bowls embodies, Line, Length and Luck.

On bad greens, you need a lot more of the latter!

❖ ❖ ❖

A bowl well sped upon its way,
May gladden you the live long day,
And make your biggest troubles small,
And life worth living after all.
While games we've won, and feats we've done,
Remembrance will recall,
That friendships made upon the green,
Are dearer than them all.

1932 • College Park BC

The club was founded by J.E. Rose and H. Payne, and the members elected Cdr. F.W. Neate as their first President and H. Payne as their first Club Captain, offices they were to hold for the first four years in order to get the club off on a good footing. Founder member J.E. Rose was elected as the Hampshire County B. A. President in 1930, and was accredited to College Park BC which would indicate that the club was affiliated to the County prior to affiliation to the Portsmouth & District B.A. The club also had the honour of proposing E. C. Smith as Hampshire President, a title he was to take up in 1968.

The land on which College Park is situated originally belonged to Winchester College. The club adopted the name of the park as their club name, and was granted permission to use the Winchester College badge as the club's blazer badge.

After affiliation to the Portsmouth & District BA in 1932, it was not too long before the club tasted its first success by winning the Division 2 title in 1933, a title they were to win again a further six times in 1950, 1955, 1959, 1973, 1979, & 1997. The Division 1 title came their way in 1944, 1953, & 1994.

During the latter years of the Second World War, W. Wade twice became the President of the District in 1944 again the following year 1945. In 1955 J. Moss became President of the Portsmouth & District Bowling Association.

Before the introduction of the Combination Leagues, the club's second team played in the lower divisions, and resulted in success when the club won the Division 3 title in 1935 & 1949. The club has many Combination titles to their name

The club has had some very good cup runs over the years and won the Rowland Cup in 1943, 1944, 1953, 1963, 1964 & 1974.

Individually club members have fared well in competitions and many Portsmouth & District titles have been won, too many to list here, but the Champion of Champions has been won in 1984 by R. Reeves, 1992 by R. Lowless, 1994 by R. Cheater and in 1998 by D. Fairall.

In the County competitions F. Neil and W. John won the Hampshire Pairs title two years running in 1958 and 1959.

In 1999 S. Fielder, C. Cooper and D. Fairall won the Two Wood Triples title.

The Secretaries Singles title has been won three times by R. Cheater in 1989, 1995 and 1996.

We cannot close this potted history of the club without mentioning the longest serving officer of College Park BC who is Robert E. Riley, who has served as Treasurer of the club since 1961, some 39 years. During this period he has also served as President for six years and as Captain for four years. Without such devoted people clubs would not be able to operate.

College Park looks forward to the new millennium in the hope of achieving more success in the various competitions in which they may enter.

1933 • Waterlooville BC

A green was constructed within the confines of the local Recreation Ground and a meeting was held at the 'Heroes of Waterloo' public house on the 9th November 1933, which was attended by 25 people interested in forming a club. The meeting was chaired by Rear Admiral H.S. Measham CMG, who was later to be elected as the club's first President. Other notable people present were Admiral O.E. Leggatt CB JP, Sir J. Timpson KBE, JP, Captain Boyle, Captain Witham and Dr D.G. Cooper.

The club was undecided whether to play Old English or EBA bowls, so it would seem that a compromise was reached and the first match, which was against the Urban District Council on Saturday 12th May 1934, was played with two rinks playing Old English rules, and two rinks playing EBA rules. The President's wife, Mrs Meacham, bowled the first wood, and to mark the occasion the President donated six jacks to the club. It is not clear whether these were Old English or EBA jacks.

In 1935 the club had the use of a pavilion, and money to furnish it was raised in many ways, and one such time was a 'Smoking Concert and Whist Drive', this raised the princely sum of 19 shillings.

A ladies section was formed in 1935 but this lapsed and did not resurrect itself again until 1961.

Confusion was in evidence that the playing of Old English and EBA. games on the same green, and the use of different types of bowls and equipment, resulted that in 1936 the club finally committed itself to the EBA. game, but it was not until 1954 that the club were to drop the words 'Old English' from their name.

The groundsman in 1936 was a Mr Newman and he continued his association with the club right up to 1969, at which time he retired. It is interesting to note that the groundsman stated that the difficulty with the green is caused by faulty foundation, which is mainly clay and is liable to crack and cause ridges.

Before the War, entertaining of visiting teams was carried out in the club's newly enlarged pavilion, and the club continued its early connections with the Heroes of Waterloo, by getting beer delivered to the green for the players refreshments.

During the War years many matches were interrupted, and the club did its bit for the War effort by converting club funds to Savings Certificates. Bowls drives were organised in aid of Salute the Soldier and Red Cross funds. To escape the bombing people moved out of Portsmouth and consequently membership increased, however when the war ended members returned to Portsmouth and the club was forced to advertise for new members.

In the early fifties the club's badge was designed, depicting an oak tree, because the green was constructed near a row of oak trees.

It was not until 1961 that the club became affiliated to the County and Portsmouth & District Associations, and in their first season in Division 3 became runners-up and gained promotion to Division 2. The club has won the Division 2 title 3 times in 1986, 1989 & 1998 and were runners up twice. They also won the Division 3 title in 1966.

The club had the honour of proposing three Presidents of the Portsmouth & District BA: 1976 J. W. Woolven, 1982 A. Gundry and in the millennium year 2000, J. Powell.

1934 • Co-operative BC

During the early 1930s, employees of the Portsea Island Co-operative Society were obviously engaged in playing bowls with other clubs in the City. It was in 1934 that Senior Management Officials decided that it would be a good idea to form a club. This was done with the help of Mr. J.H. Mihell, and Mr. G. Bailey. The club was formed and adopted the name PIMCO Managers, and commenced playing at Alexandra Park. Mr. J.H. Mihell was appointed the clubs first President.

After the Second World War the club changed its name to Co-operative BC, and continued to play at Alexandra Park until 1968 when the club decided to move to College Park where they continue to play to this day.

In 1952 and 1953 Portsmouth Co-operative BC member Capt. J. Stout, MM, with the support of the club became the President of the Portsmouth & District Bowling Association, and again gave him their support when in 1960 he became President of the Hampshire County Bowling Association.

Although never attaining great heights in the district leagues, the club did win the Division 3 title in 1960, 1962, 1980, and again in 1985.

1934 • Cosham BC

A meeting between local Shopkeepers, businessmen and councillors took place on Wednesday 8th August 1934 at the Portsbridge Hotel, and with a membership of 27 Cosham Bowling Club was conceived. The subscription for that year was agreed upon at 2/- and an annual season ticket was purchased by the membership at a cost of 7/6d.

The first President was T. Knowlys-Parr who lived at Wymering Manor and presented to the club three silver trophies one of which was named the Wymering Manor Trophy and all proceeds went to charity. J.G. Hogan was elected as Captain. The club played its first friendly match within three days of opening against Waterlooville. The club affiliated to the Portsmouth & District B.A. in October 1934. In 1935 the club entered the P&D League Division 3 and by 1938 had gained promotion to Division 1.

The design of the club's blazer badge reflects the club's proximity to the Hilsea Ramparts, which was part of the city's defence fortifications, together with the Portsmouth City crest and the Hampshire Rose.

Cosham's most illustrious past member must surely be Keith Cross (see separate article), who with his father Conyngham P. Cross were among the founder members of the club. C.P. Cross, JP was Hampshire County President in 1939 and held that title until 1944. Keith won many club titles and open titles and with his father won numerous pairs titles. C.F. Hearsey was Hampshire County President in 1972.

The Portsmouth & District Presidency has been held by the following Cosham members. 1941 and 1942 G.F. Smith, 1959 E.S. Hill, 1963 C.F. Hearsey, 1967 H. Foster, 1995 W. Lamb, and 1997 W. Luff.

The Hampshire County Fours title was won in 1966 by D. Peddie, H. Morphy, A. Parkhurst, and D. Godfrey. 1966 was also a good year for the club in P&D competitions. J. Hindley won the singles, Parkhurst, Morphy, and Hobbs won the triples, Cooper Hindley, Jones, and Butterfield won the fours, and F. Cooper won the Southsea Open singles title. More recently J. Rawlings won the Champion of Champions in 1996.

The club has won the League Division 1 title in 1960, and was runners up in that league on six other occasions. The club have also won some of the lower league titles, in 1937, 1952 & 1958 they won the League Division 2 title, and in 1936, 1957, and 1990 won the League Division 3 title. In 1939 Cosham became the proud holders of the Mayors Charity Shield.

Today Cosham Bowling Club holds a steady membership of around 60 and enters three teams in the P&D BA League. Its current successes are not necessarily measured in terms of League positions but undoubtedly as a nursery club for new and inexperienced bowlers it continues to play an important role in the development of this wonderful game.

1938 • *Forton BC*

The club was formed in 1938, and elected as their first President Alderman J. F. Lee MBE in recognition of the help he gave in getting a bowling green in the Forton area of Gosport. When war broke out in 1939 the Forton Recreation ground was commandeered by the MoD for Barrage Balloon Air Defences of the area, and therefore the club had to be put on hold for duration of the war.

In 1948 the club reformed with some of the original members such as Messrs. R. Jeffrey, J. Doggett, C. Durdan, A. Cooper, Ald. Osborne, A. Robinson and the club's first President J.F. Lee.

The club has had some notable events over the years. In 1985 the pavilion was destroyed by fire and it took over three

Forton: the First Bowl on opening day.

years to get it replaced with the building now being used today. The cost at that time was £40,000. In 1994, and after much protest to the local Council, the green was re-laid.

The club run an annual charity event, which is run on the first Saturday in July, and is known as the Reg Jeffrey Memorial trophy, all proceeds of which are donated to the International Glaucoma Association.

The club has had its fair share of success over the years and has won the District League Div 3 title 3 times (in 1953, 1965 and 1995) and were runners up in 1960, 1969 and 1970. They also won the Division 4 title in 1992. In 1949 the club won the Mayor's Charities Bowling Shield. In 1962, club Secretary B. Herbert won the Hampshire Hon. Secretaries Singles title. In 1995 a mixed four from Forton won the Hampshire & Isle of Wight Mixed Fours title.

The club looks forward to the future, and has plans to expand the pavilion, to seek new members, in particular younger bowlers, and add facilities for the disabled, so that they too can join in the game of bowls.

1939-45 • *The War Years*

At the outbreak of World War 2 the 1939 season was coming to a close, which meant that most fixtures were completed in the district.

For the 1940 season the P&DBA ran a War time league in two sections Northern and Southern, but as the season progressed this was rather restricted due to the closing of all six greens along the seafront and one green in Old Portsmouth. The Southern section was abandoned and the Northern section did not complete its fixtures.

Charity exhibition matches were played between K. Cross (Cosham) and G. Wright (Southern Railway, Eastleigh), both England Internationals, and winners of the EBA singles title. These matches were 25 shot singles games. All proceeds from these matches went to the Lord Mayors Fund for the Red Cross. On one occasion Portsmouth Football Club loaned the FA Cup, which 'Pompey' had won in 1939, and this was passed around the Milton Park green to collect donations from the spectators. These matches attracted a lot of interest around the County and in one instance over 500 spectators lined the green.

The P&DBA did run competitions but the entries were very much reduced. Records show that K. Cross won the singles and three Cosham members won the triples title. The Competition Secretary at that time was F.J.H. Young of the Southsea Waverley BC.

In 1941 only six clubs took part in the P&D league, and resulted in Cosham winning the title. The P&D continued to run competitions, but the entrants were well down. J. Todd (Milton Park) won the singles, and J. Brimble and J. Todd (Milton Park) won the pairs title.

The Rowland Cup that year was won by Priory. The Eastern Division Executive of Hampshire County BA ran a Whit Monday Charity competition, and the P&D ran a similar tournament on August Bank Holiday Monday, both events were for the Lord Mayors Charity Fund.

In 1942 a proposal by the Executive of the P&DBA which read "Any club proposing to organise a tournament or bowls competition involving invitations to clubs outside their own membership, shall first obtain sanction from the Association, this principle to also apply to other Associations during the war".

After debate the resolution was altered to "shall first consult with". The motion was vehemently opposed by a number of delegates but not withstanding the resolution was finally carried at the AGM by 22 votes to 20.

An appeal was lodged and forwarded to Hampshire County BA and the EBA. The General Purposes Committee of the EBA gave a ruling "That an Associate member (in this case the P&DBA) may not interfere with the domestic policy of a constituent member of a County BA. Should such permission be necessary, the proper authority to approach or consult in the first instance is your County BA."

It was at this point that the P&DBA stated that the resolution had not meant interference with club life. There was obviously some acrimony and prompted Milton Park, Priory, Gosport, Cosham, and Southsea Castle to disaffiliate from the P&DBA, and on August 8th 1942 formed a breakaway organisation to be known as the Eastern Division of Hampshire (Portsmouth & District) County Clubs BA. These clubs were later to be joined by Southsea Waverley, Portsmouth City Police, and NALGO.

Early in 1943 a Holidays at Home movement was brought into being. The idea was "to provide pleasurable relaxation in the various realms of sport from arduous war work, and to lessen travel outside the City".

Several fixed date tournaments were arranged within the City limits, and would appear to be well supported. A Veterans competition was introduced by the new Association, as well as a league, which was won by Priory in 1943 and 1944.

Late in 1943 peace moves were afoot to bring both Associations back together, but it is not known when that happened, but one can only assume that it coincided with the cessation of hostilities in the world.

BY APPOINTMENT
TO HER MAJESTY THE QUEEN
BRICKWOODS LTD, BREWERS
PORTSMOUTH

Taste the sun go down

BRICKWOODS BEERS

1947 • *Eastney B.C.*

In 1947 employees of the Portsmouth City Transport formed a bowling club which was to be known as Passenger Transport B.C. and played at Milton Park. They continued to play right up to 1990 at which time the club had only two members who were Bus Company employees. The club's title did not reflect the membership so a meeting was called in 1990. Two names were proposed, 'Goldsmith' and 'Eastney'. It was at this meeting, that, by a majority of one vote the membership decided to change their name to Eastney. In the clubs last season as Passenger Transport they gained promotion and so Eastney started the 1991 season in League Division 2.

The first President of the club was John Breach, and C. Campbell S. Herridge, D. Biggs, M. Brown, R. Yates, J. Slatter and D. Daniels were some of the Passenger Transport members of the 1970's, and 1980's.

The clubs badge was designed around the three nautical pennants for 'E' 'B' & 'C' and the name and badge were adopted because of the clubs proximity to the sea and the Eastney Naval history.

As Passenger Transport the team won the league Division 3 title in 1951, and have been runners up on three other occasions. Eastney have been runners up twice in Division 4 in 1994 and 1998, and the Combination side won the Division 6 title in 1998.

The P&D Triples title was won in 1994 by P. Turton, R. Newell & C. Dixon.

Since 1994 the club, in conjunction with Milton Park Ladies, has held a Charity Mixed Pairs competition, which is called the Vic Robinson Day. To date the club has raised nearly £3,000 and the nominated Charity is The Rowans Hospice in Purbrook.

1948 • Lakeside BC

In 1946 Ern Bryant a Chargeman in the Dockyard, together with some of his fellow Burners, decided to play bowls on the number 3 Southsea Castle green, as a form of relaxation and just for fun.

Later they learned that the Drawing Office in the Dockyard had formed a Sunday Dockyard League. The Burners decided to apply to join, and later was accepted into the league. At this time the organisation was known as DECSA (Dockyard Establishment Central Sports Association). The players adopted the team name of Welburns, which was derived from the two trades, which made up the team, welders and burners.

In 1948 Welburns BC members decided to apply for affiliation to Hampshire County and Portsmouth & District Bowling Associations. In 1949 after the club had been affiliated they entered the P&D League Division 3. The club played at Southsea Castle for some twenty years at which time the club decided to move to Canoe Lake bowling green when one of the greens had been vacated by Milton Casuals. The move was led by Secretary Reg Mitchell who continued to hold this office until the late 1970's, at which time Bill (Nobby) Clark took over.

Nobby Clark and Alf Birt who are past Presidents of Welburns BC and were original members of the team, are still playing to date, although both have joined the neighbouring club at Canoe Lake (Star & Crescent).

The Dockyard Sports Association was wound up in 1983 and the name Welburns, which was affiliated to it, had to be changed. Various names were put forward and in the end the name Lakeside was adopted, appropriate for the team playing adjacent to the Canoe Lake complex at Southsea.

Morley Stewart-Jones took over as Secretary of the newly named club, a position that he has held to date.

The club has always been one of the smaller clubs in the City, numbers wise, but managed to maintain a first team and one Combination team, until a rule change in the league required clubs to have at least 32 registered players to enter two teams in the leagues. As the club only had 26 players it was forced to withdraw its Combination team, but in recent years with the introduction of the Mid-week triples league helped the club to give most players an opportunity of playing in the leagues.

As Welburns the club was runners up in Division 3 in 1972, and as Lakeside were runners up in Division 4 in 1987.

Most success has been gained by the club in the Mid-week triples league. They won the Town section in 1997 and again the following year 1998, and were runners up in this section in 1999.

1949 • *Highbury BC*

The Founder members of the club were M.M. Beveridge, C. O. Connor, E.V. Hill, L. Quarton, J. Shrubb, and S.A. Tout. The first President elected was L. Quarton.

It took only four years for the club to win its first league title, and gain promotion to the 2nd Division. Further honours for the club has been Division 2 winners in 1960, Division 3 winners in 1968 and again in 1976, Division 4 winners in 1997. They have been runners up in Division 2. In 1958, 1972, and 1986, and runners up in Division 3 in 1982.

Individual club members have also gained honours, and K. Leader won the Portsmouth & District singles title in 1981,

Two former presidents, Brian Ivemey and Ivan Robb, standing in front of the Highbury Clubhouse, formally a ticket office for the Portsdown to Horndean light railway.

but a high was reached in 1963 when E. Hill and R. Dickie won the Hampshire County pairs title, and went on to represent the County at the National Finals.

The club has had had the honour over the years of proposing no less than five club members as President of the Portsmouth & District, who were duly elected. They are 1964 A.V. Organ, 1977 A.A. Haigh, 1984 A. Bowen, 1987 R. Cooper, and 1996 I. Robb.

The club has always played at their present green, which now forms part of the Cosham Park Bowling Association, and they lease the green from the Portsmouth City Council.

The corrugated iron roofed building which stands alongside the Highbury green, originally started life as a Ticket Office for the Portsdown to Horndean Light Railway. It now serves as the clubhouse for Highbury BC, and you may be surprised to know that it is a listed building.

1950 • *Gas Social B.C.*

Such was the enthusiasm of Gas Company employees who worked at the Flathouse Works, which is now the site of the Continental Ferry Port, that they formed a bowls club and started life known as Portsmouth Gas Undertaking BC, and played initially at Pembroke Gardens and later at Southsea Castle, however the club finally settled on the Alexandra Park greens in Northern Parade, where they currently play.

The Gas Company encouraged employees to join the social side of the company, which included founder bowls members W. Sexton who worked as a Pressure man, G. Goddard a Timekeeper, R. Cairncross a Shift Foreman, and E. Lockley a Carpenters mate. E. Lockley was the club's team captain in the early days of formation. For a long while only Gas Company employees were allowed to play bowls for the club.

In 1951 after the club had been affiliated to the County and District Associations, they entered a team in the P&D League Division 3.

In 1968 the club changed their title to Southern Gas Undertaking (Portsmouth), and the club had better fortunes with that name, and won the Division 3 title three times in 1961, 1969 and 1972, and were runners up in that Division in 1967, 1968, 1971 and 1975. Obviously the club gained promotion to Division 2 but was soon relegated and went down to the lower division. The club currently plays in Division 4, but hope for better things in the future.

In 1982 the club changed its name to Gas Social BC, and even now over half of the membership are either employed by or are retired from British Gas.

1961 • Bridgemary B.C.

In the early 1960's the area had grown to such an extent that Councillor J. (Sid) Seymour persuaded the Gosport Borough Council to build a bowling green in Bridgemary. This was completed in 1968, and on May 31st 1969 the Mayor of Gosport, Councillor Cooley opened the green.

The club was formed as a mixed bowling club and its first President of the club was Councillor Seymour, this was in recognition of all the help and assistance given to the club over the years during the clubs formation.

The origin of the clubs badge lies in the geographical location of the club. The site is close to the former home of a prominent and historical family named Prideaux-Brune. In June 1969 the Founder President sought and obtained permission of Lady Prideaux-Brune to use their Families of Arms as the basis of a design for the clubs badge, and is an adaptation of the second and third quarterlies of the Prideaux-Brune Coat of Arms.

The club became affiliated to Hampshire County & District B. A. and entered the District leagues, and in 1973 won the Division 3 title, and again won that title in 1979. They have also won the Division 4 title twice in 1991 and 1998.

The club has had many individual successes over the years, in particular P. Kemp who won the Hampshire County Hon. Secretaries Singles title in 1976.

The club has a membership of 120, with a Junior Section. The club has in addition four Partially Sighted Members and their Carers.

In 1989 the club became a private club and now leases the facilities from the Gosport Borough Council.

1963 • Naismith B.C.

A bowling club was formed by the employees of C.J.C. Developments, an engineering firm based in Farlington, North Portsmouth. For the first two years the club played only friendly games. The club was known at that time as CJC Developments and played at various venues around the City. Some of the founder members included John Bartlett, Alf Nother, Sid Newdenny and Bill Bouth. At the club's first meeting Bill Bouth was elected the club's first President.

As the membership grew, the members decided to apply to enter the Portsmouth & District leagues and started to play on the nearby green at Drayton Park. At this time the club decided to call themselves Drayton Park and played there from 1965 up to 1970.

In 1970 a gentleman by the name of Casell, who owned an engineering drawing office firm called Naismith, based in the Airspeed complex on the Eastern Road, decided that he would support the club. It was decided to move from Drayton Park to the Copnor Bridge green and rename the club Naismith B.C. The club has continued to play at Copnor to this day.

All clubs need officers, and Jim Bartlett has served as club Secretary since 1971; on top of this duty Jim has been the Portsmouth & District Match Secretary for the last 6 years.

The club won the District League Division 3 title in 1975, and have been runners up in that league 4 times in 1974, 1978, 1986 and 1994. The club gained promotion to Division 2, but was unable to sustain its position and currently plays in Division 3.

The club has had Champion of Champion winners over the years: Ron Cummings in 1981, John Knowles in 1991 and Malcolm Wake in 1999.

1965 • Leigh Park BC

A Bowling Green was built by Havant Borough Council to serve those people living in Leigh Park. Early in 1965, Bert Corbin and George Proctor (a Councillor of the Havant Borough Council) met and decided to endeavour to find people in the vicinity who may be interested in forming a Bowling club. All sorts of advertising was undertaken to enlighten the local population of the existence of the Bowling Green in the park. Eventually, enough people were interested and a committee was formed headed by Chairman/President A. Hunt; G. Proctor was elected Secretary and B. Corbin was elected Treasurer.

The opening of the green was on a Whit Sunday, 26th May and the first bowl was bowled by Joan Corbin acting in her position as wife of the Chief Officer of Police for the District. The opening was a low-key affair, due to the fact that the membership at that time amounted to only twelve people.

The Havant Police Sports Club helped to boost the membership, but the club still had difficulty in attracting new members. With the lack of membership the club negotiated a reduction in the rent, until such time as the club could become financially viable.

By 1975, membership had increased to such an extent that the club decided to enter the Portsmouth & District Bowling Association league. In its first league season in Division 3 the club were runners up to Highbury by only two points. The following season they went one better and gained promotion to Division 2. In 1981 the club won the Division 2 title and was promoted to Division 1. Their highest position in the league to date was to be runners up in Division 1 in 1987 and 1990. The club has also won the Division 2 title on two other occasions: in 1985 and 1993. In 1986 Leigh Park won the Rowland Cup.

Individually members have won District titles and in 1985 John Mackney was runner up in the Hampshire County singles and went on to represent the County at National level.

The club had a good year in 1989 when they reached the final of the County Club Championship, losing in the final to Boscombe Cliff.

Initially, in 1966 the club had no clubhouse or accommodation, and in 1967 the members erected a large garden shed as a stopgap. In later years a permanent clubhouse was built and the club could boast that it was the best in the district. In 1989 a bar was added for social purposes and the entertaining of visiting teams; this proved a great success due to the efforts of Arthur and Doris Suter and Billy Beard.

In 1994/95 further improvements to the clubhouse were made including the kitchen, facilities for the disabled and additional toilets. The club is looking to further improve the facilities by providing changing rooms within the complex of the green area.

The club looks forward to the future and is known as "The Friendly Club in the Park".

1969 • Portsmouth Water Company B.C.

The club was formed as a section of the Portsmouth Water Company Sports & Social Club. On completion of the construction of the Bowls Green at the Company's Head Office at Brockhampton Springs in Havant, the club played as a friendly team throughout the seventies, led by founder member Stan Drew and ably assisted by Dorothy Cooper.

The club soon became a popular venue for matches with other clubs as the green is surrounded by lakes, fields and flowerbeds.

Roy Jones was one of the prime movers in 1978 when the club became affiliated to the Hampshire County BA, and the Portsmouth & District BA, at which time the Company agreed to have the green extended to allow competition bowls to be played. The club entered the Portsmouth & District League 3 in 1981 and in 1984 the club won the Division 3 title and gained promotion to Division 2. The following year they were runners up in Division 2 and found themselves in Division 1 after a very short space of time. The club remained in the top division for eight years.

After some fluctuation in the club's fortunes it has gained promotion to the top division for the Portsmouth & Districts 75th anniversary year.

In the late eighties there was a surge of interest in bowls amongst Social Club members, which prompted the Bowls Section to enter a second team in the Combination League. Progress has been steady and in the early nineties the 'Combo' team had a season with a 100% record and have steadily moved up to the Combination 2 league.

Portsmouth Water BC were Rowland Cup Finalists in 1983 and 1996, losing on both occasions to Civil Service BC. The club also reached the County Club Divisional Final in 1991, losing again to Civil Service BC.

Individually, club members have been successful: in 1987 D. Bowerman and S. Chandler won the Southsea Open Pairs title. The Southsea Open Triples title was won in 1989 by D. Bowerman, C. Wilton and S. Filippi (IBM) and in 1997 by D. Walker, M. Leeson, and K. Wright.

The club had the honour of nominating Terry Stone-Houghton as President of the Portsmouth & District Bowling Association, a position that he was to hold in 1993. In 1994 Terry became the Senior Vice President of the Hampshire County Bowling Association and in the following year became the Deputy President for the County.

The club continues to be an excellent venue for Bowls, hosting two Portsmouth & District matches per season and holding two Charity events each year, which are well supported by bowlers from other clubs from the P&D.

The recent installation of an Automatic Irrigation System and the continued support from the Social Club Committee should help to ensure a healthy future for the Portsmouth Water Company Bowls Club.

1970 • Rowner B.C.

The Rowner Bowling Club was formed by a group of enthusiasts in 1970, and George Giles was elected as their first President. The green was laid by the Gosport Borough Council and is leased to the Rowner BC.

In 1977 and 1991 the club won the League Division 2 title, and in 1971 and 1986 won the League Division 3 top spot. Included in Rowners achievements was the winning of the Rowland Cup in 1995.

In 1976, C. Freeman, C. Giles and T. Grant won the County Triples title and went on to represent Hampshire at the EBA Championships.

The club has given good support to Portsmouth & District BA over the years and has hosted many representative matches for the district.

The club's badge depicts Fort Rowner, one of the 'Palmeston Follies', with Royal Air Force wings, which represents the time when the area was an RAF airfield (RAF Grange). In the foreground is a Viking galleon representing the arrival of the Bishop of Winchester in AD 1140 to Gosport ('Gods Port').

1972 • IBM Bowls Club

In 1972, a group of IBM colleagues (Hugh Davies, Andy Crocker, Edwin Humphries and Peter Greenhill) who worked at the Northern Road building, started to use the facilities of the Highbury green during their summer lunchtimes. Their interest grew to such an extent that it attracted enough like-minded enthusiasts to enable them to form a team.

The first President was Peter Greenhill, and the newly formed IBM Bowls Club became affiliated to the County and District Bowling Associations allowing the club to enter the P&D League Division 3.

Initially, the club played at Drayton Park, which was to be the scene of many a defeat, but this harsh introduction helped educate the founder members in the subtleties of this glorious game. In the late seventies the club moved to their present green in Northern Parade, and this heralded a change of fortunes when in 1982 the club won the league and was promoted to Division 2. In 1987 they won the Division 2 title thus gaining promotion to Division 1.

The club has won the Division 1 title twice; in 1991 and 1995. Other club achievements include winning the Rowland Cup in 1990, 1992 & 1999, and the Eastern Division County Club title in 1994 and 1996.

Individual honours have been many: M. Hanson, P. Faulkner, T. Pullin & I. Foster won the Hampshire County fours title in 1994 and went on to represent the County at the National Finals in Worthing. S. Filippi (1985) and M. Parker (1994) have both won the Southsea Open Singles title, M. Hanson & B. Sidebottom won the P&D Pairs title in 1994 and in 1999 S. Robertson represented England in the U-25 Indoor International matches.

The club has always been open to all and, over the years, has had the good fortune to be able to attract a number of County standard bowlers into its ranks. The IBM Bowls Club is extremely proud to have at least one club representative in the Hampshire Middleton Cup Team for each of the last six years. These members include I. Foster, B. Sidebottom, P. Hobday, M. Hanson and S. Robertson.

In 1992 the club had the honour of proposing and supporting Dave Wildman as President of the Portsmouth & District BA during his term in office.

The club has its own Internet website, which includes photographs of members past and present and a record of fixtures and results from the recent past. See it at:

www. geocities. com/Colosseum/Rink/2455/IBMBC.html

The A B C of Bowls

A = Ability

B = Bottle

C = Compatability

1974 • Fareham BC

Unlike most other clubs, whereby bowlers form a club before the green is built, Fareham Borough Council laid a bowling green in the Park Lane Recreation Ground and then advertised for someone to organise a bowling club. The response was very good and among the many replies was one from C.F. Hearsay, who in 1972 was President of the Hampshire County Bowling Association. Obviously with Bert Hearsay's experience and other interested bowlers, the Fareham Bowling Club was formed as a mixed club and at the start of the 1974 season the green was officially opened by Mrs Gardner, the Mayor of Fareham, with some 50 people in attendance.

So popular was the club, which clearly fulfilled a need in the Fareham area, that numbers soon increased and the club currently has 100 gentlemen and 70 lady members.

In 1997 the club was runner up in League Division 2 and gained promotion to Division 1. Earlier successes included winning the Division 3 title four times in 1981, 1983, 1987 & 1992 and being runners-up in that league in 1977 and 1980.

The club had the honour of proposing T. Bayliss as President of the Hampshire County Bowling Association in 1988 and celebrated his appointment with a match against a team representing the County.

In recent years the club has improved the clubhouse and the facilities therein with the aid of grants of £21,450 from the Lottery Sports Council and £16,500 from the Foundation for Sports and Arts.

Individual honours have been many in the District competitions, but this was capped in 1994 when Charles Bailey aided and abetted by his wife Rosemary captured the

National Mixed Pairs title which was sponsored by Ashbourne Homes.

In the same year Charles Bailey and Ken Ford assisted by their wives, the two Rosemarys, became runners up in the National Mixed Fours title which was sponsored by Teachers Whiskey. I trust they were duly rewarded by the sponsor for their celebratory drink.

Don't put on 'Bias'— go straight for

JOHNNIE WALKER

Born 1820—still going Strong

BOWLING DOWN THE YEARS

1976 • *Vosper Thornycroft BC*

In 1976, a group of employees from the Vosper Thornycroft Controls Division at Cosham got together and formed a bowls club. The only person with bowls experience and the prime person to get the club up and running was Cyril Kaye.

At the club's first meeting the membership elected Arthur Jaimeson as President. Some of the current members who were at that meeting are John Ralphs, Tony Berridge, Dave Harding, and Peter Matthews.

The club affiliated to the County and District Associations, and decided to play at Drayton Park, later they moved to Alexandra Park in 1981 and currently still play there.

The club entered League Division 3. It was not too long before they gained promotion to Division 2 by winning the title in 1978. This was to be repeated again in 1988 and 1991; they were also runners up in that league in 1985. The club was runner up in Division 2 in 1993 and 1995 and was promoted to Division 1. In 1995 they were runners up in the Rowland Cup.

The club seems to jump between divisions – their longest stay in the top league was between 1996-1999 – unfortunately in 1999 they were relegated back to Division 2.

Individually, club members have won their share of trophies, notably in 1995 when K. Reilly, D. Harding & P. Sansbury won the P&D triples title. D. Harding and K. Leader have also won the Champion of Champions title.

The club looks forward to the future and perhaps, who knows, to a longer stay in Division 1 next time!

1977 • Hayling Island BC

Vi Young who was an experienced bowler, with husband Maurice, and Bill Biggs, who was also an experienced bowler, called a meeting with Messrs. Macfadyan, Sparham, Baugham, Green, Miles, McCuiver, and Bryant, and became the nucleus of the founder members. They all decided to meet on the 23rd June 1977 and a committee was formed headed by Vi Young, later she was elected the first President of the club. It was formed as a mixed club. The club very soon had 50 members.

The six rink green had been built by the Havant Borough Council, and it is interesting to note that the first year's rent for 4 rinks was just £152, though should the club require additional rinks these would be available at extra cost. Membership fees for the year were set at £5 per annum. The clubhouse was a Portakabin, which stood alongside the green. For entertaining visiting teams the club hired the Girl Guides hut which was across the other side of the park. It was not until the Community Centre was built that accommodation was on a more permanent basis. This consisted of a small room within the Centre complex. In 1996 the Council built a more comprehensive clubhouse, however this was still attached to the Community Centre.

In the early years the club was very much a social club, and most of the new members borrowed lignum woods which were available from the Council, Many social activities took place away from the green in order to raise funds for the club, and it was not until 1979 that the club decided to apply for affiliation to the Portsmouth & District and Hampshire County Bowling Associations. The club entered the P&D League 3 and it was in 1984 that they gained promotion to League Division 2

The clubs badge features four keys, which represents the historical background of the four ancient Parishes on the island: St. Marys, St. Peters, St. Andrews, and St. Patricks.

In 1995 the club won promotion from Division 2 to Division 1 of the P&D League, and remained there for two seasons. In 1990 they won the Division 4 Title.

The club boasts that it was here on Hayling that two local youngsters learnt their skills and went on to better things.

D. Bishop went on to become the County singles Champion in 1990. Both D. Bishop and M. Hanson represented the County in the Middleton Cup, as well as winning numerous other titles.

Individual honours have been many notably A. Locke who won the Littlehampton Open singles title in 1982 and again at the age of 72 in 1987. R. Gunter also won this title in 1991.

In 1997 K. Brown, G. Thomas, P. Bolter, and R. Gunter won the Portsmouth & District fours title. R. King won the P&D over 60 singles title in 1991

In 1992 R. Edmonds became the President of the Hampshire County B. A., a position that he was to repeat again in 1996.

Hayling Island BC: A.Bowen and H.McCullie raising the flag in 1980.

BOWLING DOWN THE YEARS · **69**

1979 • Lee on the Solent

In 1979 a group of 58 Lee on the Solent residents formed a bowling club, and elected C. Ford as their first President. Although they did not have a green of their own in the vicinity, they were not deterred, and arranged to bowl on a very limited basis initially on the Forton green in Gosport, and at a later date at the Bridgemary club.

Some of the early founder members still with the club to date are, Peter & Joan Titheridge, Millie Carter, Fred Jones, John Rae, Jean Minter, Doreen Turner, and Irene Bell to name but a few.

The joining fee was 10p, and the annual subscription was fixed at £14.

Many representations to have a bowling green for the Lee on the Solent residents was made to Gosport Borough Council, even the Member of Parliament, and some local Councillors gave support, but the Council adopted a delaying tactic. During all this time the club grew in strength and could boast the largest membership of any club in the Gosport area.

At that time John Colbourn the Secretary organised a petition and collected some 600 signatures from local residents and presented the petition to the Gosport Borough Council. After much protracted negotiations a site in the corner of the recreation ground was allocated next to the cricket pavilion.

Having had the ground allotted the members put in a lot of hard work, such as coffee mornings, raffles etc, and undertook various other ways of raising money, Nearby local clubs made an effort and contributed to the fund which slowly but steadily built up for the construction of the green. Loans were obtained and donations from members ranging from £100 to £2000. 00 were given.

After many setbacks and inflated prices from some contractors a fairer and more acceptable price was obtained from a company in the North of England, and eventually the green was laid.

Thanks to the driving force of John Colbourn and the undivided support of the members, the Lee on the Solent green was officially opened in April 1985, and as a gesture of thanks to all the clubs who had supported them during their long and protracted efforts to get a bowling green in the area, six teams were invited along for the opening days bowling event.

Lee on the Solent BC: A working Party of founder members.

The club had a lot of debts to finance, and due to careful management by the committees over the years the club now find themselves on a good financial footing.

The club won promotion to the Portsmouth & District League Division 2 in 1998 when they won league Div 3, a title that they also won in 1994. They have also won the Division 4 title in 1986.

The Competitor
"I only play for enjoyment ... the main part of which is winning." *DB*

❖ ❖ ❖

The Boaster
"My bowls have suffered so much chalk damage." DB

❖ ❖ ❖

The Heavy Bowler
"You're slightly in the ditch." DB

❖ ❖ ❖

The Mathematician
"I don't mind who wins provided we have more shots on the card." DB

❖ ❖ ❖

The Realist
When asked your handicap, 'being married' will not be taken as a satisfactory answer. DB

1980 Crofton BC

In 1979 the Fareham Borough Council constructed a bowling green alongside the Crofton Community Centre and invited people in the Stubbington area to form a bowls club.

A meeting was held in the Community Centre on 29th May 1980, and over 100 local people attended. A committee was formed to organise the club. The first President was Norman Jones, the Secretary was Dorrine Burton-Jenkins and the Treasurer was George Woodiwise. The club was formed as a mixed club and the name was to be Stubbington Bowls Club.

In July 1980 the Mayor of Fareham Mrs Rosemary Pockley officially opened the green, and she requested that the club be known as Crofton Bowls Club.

The first year attracted 120 members, but only a few had experience in bowling, and it was those members who set out to teach the newcomers the rudiments of the game.

There was no clubhouse or toilet facilities in those days and being alongside the Community Centre members had to use the Centre and if that was closed make the trek to the toilet facilities in the village.

In 1981 the club undertook to entertain visiting teams in friendly matches, but found that difficult due to the lack of facilities.

In 1982 the club decided to seek permission to erect a pavilion, this was granted and by the following season the club had raised enough money from raffles, coffee mornings, bring and buy sales etc; to purchased a wooden building from a local firm. Members set about digging the foundations for the new facility. After the pavilion was erected, volunteers decorated and fitted it out.

Since the first building in 1983 two more extensions have been added, the final one in 1997 when the ladies toilets were re-sited, and a large kitchen facility was added, and at the same time a separate building was erected to house the men's changing room and toilet. The entire finance for all of these projects was paid for from club funds, which had been raised by Club Members.

In 1984 the club entered the Portsmouth & District league, and it was in 1987 that the club gained its first honour by winning the Division 4 title and gained promotion to Division 3, and eventually to Division 2.

The club currently play four teams in the Gosport & Fareham Mixed Triples League, and teams in the ladies and men's leagues of the Portsmouth & District.

Good Etiquette
"In mixed play, a gentleman will always raise his hat before firing a lady's bowl out of the head." DB

❖ ❖ ❖

Over Statement
"I meant an Imperial yard, not a shipyard." DB

❖ ❖ ❖

The Midwife
"It's the wrong line, wrong weight ... but a beautiful delivery." DB

❖ ❖ ❖

Optical Illusion
"It's not a tied end ...
... our bowl is touching more than yours!"

1982 • *Purbrook Heath BC*

Purbrook Heath BC was formed as a mixed bowling club, and the first meeting took place on the 25th March 1982, chaired by Councillor Timothy Williams, to fulfill the needs of bowlers both experienced and new, in this fast developing area south of Waterlooville. Councillor Williams reported that he had spent the last 15 years pressing the Havant Council for a green at Purbrook. Other founder members included G. Meaden, R. Keyworth, F. Barge, J. Davis, Mrs. P. Davis, Mrs. Keyworth, and J. Fox.

The green was built by the Havant Borough Council, and was opened on 1st May 1982. Initially the green was enclosed with the traditional wind break hedging around the perimeter, but due to vandalism of the green a wire fence had to be erected to safeguard the playing area. The clubhouse was the standard issue Portakabin supplied by the Havant council. The present brick built pavilion was the first to be built by the council, since when the design has been altered for the better. The club is currently trying to get some improvements done to the building.

The club's blazer badge depicts the Purbrook Heath Brook.

At the District AGM, G. Meaden was proposed by Purbrook Heath, to the position of Portsmouth & District President, and was elected to that office in 1990. In recent years the club has provided other Executive Officers in the District, notably J. Powell, Treasurer, and G. Hannah League Secretary. To mark their years in office G. Meaden presented the Combination 5 winners Shield, and G. Hannah presented the Combination 6 runners up Shield to the Portsmouth & District Bowling Association.

The club has had some success in the district leagues, and won the Division 3 title in 1997, and were runners up in Division 4 in 1988 and 1990.

The club although being fairly young, is very active and has achieved its initial aim to provide bowling in the area, and as a mark of his achievement Timothy Williams was made a Life President.

The club is close to the Rowans Hospice and in recent years has donated money to this worth while organisation.

Purbrook Heath BC: the first purpose built brick pavilion in the Borough Of Havant area.

1984 • *Bedhampton BC*

For many years Havant Councillor Bill Yeoman stressed the need for an additional bowling green in the Havant area to cope with the ever increasing numbers of people in the area wanting to play bowls. After ten years of persistence, and getting the nod from the Havant Borough Council, Bill Yeoman called an inaugural meeting of the club on the 3rd October 1983. This was soon followed by the club's first General Meeting on the 9th January 1984. 150 people applied to become members and the club was formed as a mixed club.

The first honour for the club was the runner up spot in Division 4 and it was a proud occasion for the club when Eric Googe stepped forward to collect the trophy. Further honours

Bedhampton BC, opened by the Mayor of Havant.

were forthcoming when the club won the Division 4 title in 1989, 1995 and 1999.

The ladies section joined the P&DWBA leagues in 1987.

Portacabins were the standard issue for bowling clubs in the Havant area, and founder members put in a lot of work to improve the facility to be able to seat 6 rinks at tea and also provide a veranda for viewing the games in progress. A kitchen was constructed and fitted out by George Hall. In 1995 the club was provided with a brick built Pavilion by the Havant Borough Council.

The club is strong and vigorous, and looks to the future with optimism.

Clean Living
"It's leading a good life that brings good luck."

❖ ❖ ❖

Relief (after a lucky shot)
"I thought for a minute that you had missed it."

❖ ❖ ❖

The Fisherman
"You are as thin as a kipper."

❖ ❖ ❖

Salacious
"You are as thin as a honeymoon nightie ...
... but not half as exciting!"

1985 • *Portsmouth Post Office BC*

In the early 1980's interest was shown by several Postmen in the Portsmouth Sorting Office, and was fascinated by the game of bowls. During a canteen break Ted Winning, who at that time was playing for the Civil Service was asked to show those who were interested how to play the game.

Ted, with Bob Partridge and Ray Golding both of whom also played at the Civil Service, arranged to book two rinks at Milton Park, expecting only a few to turn up. Much to their surprise over 40 Postmen came along that afternoon, too many for the two rinks that had been booked. However two rinks were booked for two days later and this time over 35 Postmen appeared. This was the beginning of Portsmouth Post Office BC.

With so much interest Ted was asked to make some enquiries at the City Council Offices to see if the Postmen could get the use of a green. As it happened the Welburns BC had just moved along the seafront to Canoe Lake and left number 3 green available at Southsea Castle. The green was offered to the Post Office, which they readily took, and the club still plays there to this day.

At the clubs first official meeting Bob Partridge was elected the clubs first President, and Ted Winning the clubs Captain.

A great deal of help and support was given by the Post Office Sports & Social Club to get the bowling section off the ground and even paid for six sets of bowls for use by the members.

The club became affiliated in 1985, which allowed them to enter the District league Division 3, and within a few short years won the Division 3 title in 1989. This was to be repeated again in 1999. In 1988 the club won the Division 4 title.

The club is in the main all Postmen, and has two teams in the leagues. Having just won the Division 3 title the club looks forward to competing in Division 2 in the millennium year.

Every year the club organises a Charity event, which is well supported, and money is raised for good causes.

The Bombardier
"Just draw - leave the firing to me."

❖ ❖ ❖

Sardonic
"I thought you were playing on this rink."

❖ ❖ ❖

Trauma
"You've improved it worse."

❖ ❖ ❖

The Cynic
"Everything in our favour is against us."

❖ ❖ ❖

Cryptic
"One more each end and we're equal."

1986 • Drayton Park

Est. 1986

Formed by a small but enthusiastic group of bowlers who wished to take advantage of the fairly new facilities in Drayton Park.

The first President was Mr. John Slate, and early members included Gordon Tilbury, John Young, and Alf Foster.

The clubs Logo is a single fouled anchor which is not an indication of its Naval connections, but rather of the founders wishes that the club be set on a firm and steady foundation, however some of the present club members do have a strong Naval connection.

Being a mixed club the ladies have played their part in district bowls, notably Judy Goldman who was the P&D

Draton Park: some early members in 1988.

BOWLING DOWN THE YEARS · 81

Ladies President in 1991, and was Secretary of P&DWBA for three years.

Although not achieving honours in the main leagues, the club gained promotion to Combination Division 4 in 1991, and followed this with winning Combination Division 4 in 1992. Jeff Amos reached the semi-finals of the District Champion of Champions in 1997 & 1998.

The club has a current membership of 114, which enables the club to arrange tours to various parts of the Country. To celebrate the millennium the club intends to tour the Costa Del Sol.

The club has a long lease from the Portsmouth City Council for the Green and Pavilion, and collect fees for the Council for the use of the facilities.

Definitions

An Optimist...

is a player who turns up to play a game of Bowls without his wet gear.

❖ ❖ ❖

A Pessimist...

is a player who wears a belt as well as braces.

❖ ❖ ❖

A Committee...

is a body that keeps minutes, but wastes hours.

1986 • Portchester BC

The clubs early days in 1983 found members playing short mat bowls in the Portchester Community Association hall.

In 1986 the Fareham Borough Council installed a Matchmaker artificial surface green in the Community Association grounds. A public meeting was called which was attended not only by the short mat bowlers but many other people interested in the game of bowls. It was decided at this meeting to form the Portchester Bowling Club, and to operate it as a mixed club.

The first President recorded is J. Doggett, followed by J. Harrison in 1990-91, and then in 1992 to date by Bert Cox.

Before the club could enter competitive bowls the club had to be affiliated to the Hampshire County and Portsmouth & District Bowling Associations, and in order to apply the 'green' had to be inspected to see if it came up to E. B. A. standards. This was done and it came through the inspection with flying colours. The club immediately entered a team in the P&D League Division 4.

The Pavilion was built with the assistance of grants from the Fareham Borough Council, Hampshire Playing Fields Association, and by funds raised by the Portchester BC members.

It is a fact that some clubs are less than enthusiastic when having to play on the artificial surface green, but they quickly adjust to the fast running and wide drawing rinks and some keenly contested matches are played.

The club has gone from strength to strength over the years and can boast a current membership of 120. The club has been the starting point for some notable bowlers in the district, but they have left the club for pastures new, that is to say non artificial greens, however the club finds that the fast green allows younger people and handicapped people to try the game without too much effort.

After 12 years use the green is now showing its age, and the club is currently negotiating with the Fareham Borough Council for a replacement green. Since the green was laid there have been vast improvements in artificial green manufacture.

The club adopted as its club badge a circle with the outline of the nearby Portchester Castle Keep in the centre.

The club was proud to host a visit from the Hampshire County B.A. President Richard Edmonds and his team in 1992, a match, which most members who were present remember.

Portchester gained promotion to League Division 3 in 1996, but unfortunately were relegated in the 1999 season and will start the new millennium in Division 4.

At this point mention must be made of those long serving Committee members without whom clubs could not function, such as H. Cox who was elected the clubs first and only Secretary to date, and R. Jones who was Treasurer for over 10 years.

1989 Cowplain BC

In the late 1970's Havant Borough Councillor Alderman J. Carruthers was pressing the Council for a bowling green in Cowplain. Eventually in 1987 a green was constructed in the Padnell Road Recreation Ground. In 1988 W. Hellier who was Chairman of the Cowplain Activities Centre was asked to advertise the new facility, with a view to forming a bowling club. After several meetings and much hard work by local bowling enthusiasts a mixed bowling club was formed with 120 members. The first President was W. Hellier, who later became President of Portsmouth & District B. A. in 1994.

The green was officially opened in April 1989 by the Mayor of Havant P. Osbourne, who bowled the first bowl.

During the early years the club had a reputation for friendliness and hospitality, and has always had a waiting list of applicants wanting to join the club. In those days the club had the use of a Portakabin sited alongside the green, with the added facilities of the Activities Centre. This was far from satisfactory and with the help of local Councillors a new pavilion costing £140,000 was constructed in 1995 and the club can boast that it is the best in the Havant Borough district.

In 1989 the club became affiliated to the Hampshire County and Portsmouth & District Bowling Associations and as a result were able to enter the P&D league Division 4 for the 1990 season. In 1993 the club won the Division 4 title, and in 1998 became runners up in Division 3 and were promoted to Division 2. The club has two Combination teams playing in the District leagues. The highlight came for the club in 1999 when they reached the local final of the County Club Championship losing out to Portsmouth Civil Service who were the ultimate winners of the County Championship.

1990 • Denmead BC

In the Middle 1980's David Banting went around the village to collect names of people interested in a Bowling Green in Denmead. After 5 years and on June 12th 1990 a meeting was called to discuss this project. 65 ladies and gentlemen attended. Prominent among these was Stan & Dorothy Cadman, Pat Lee, Ron & Margaret Thomas, George Hazzard, Keith May, Ken Morgon, and Fred Ketley. Each person attending this meeting paid £2. into a fund for administrative expenses. A mixed Committee was formed to further the reality of Demead BC Stan Cadman was elected Chairman.

Initially the project was a joint venture between Denmead BC and the Parish Council, which had set up a sub-committee of the Parish Council under the Chairmanship of Peter Goodman, aided by Doug Hill a permanent member of the Council.

Much activity took place to raise money, and Pat Lee wrote 57 letters to various firms and organisations, asking for their support, notably Biltons the builders, Lloyds Bank, Southern Television etc. : Winchester City Council gave £25,000, the Parish Council £10,000, the Hampshire Playing Fields Association £2,000, local businesses contributed and the members raised a further £1,000 for the fund.

The Parish Council agreed to lease the land for 99 years at a peppercorn rent. By July 1991 sufficient funds had been raised to make a start on laying the green. Havant Borough Council completed this in October 1991 at a cost of £39,000.

At this time membership had increased to 100, many of whom, led by Pamela Atkinson, were involved in landscaping the surrounding area.

The first clubhouse was an old caravan purchased for £50. and was used throughout the first season. Councillor Mike Read bowled the first bowl, in May 1992.

The caravan was replaced in 1993 with a Portakabin at a cost of £1,500. Ever mindful of the need of a more permanent pavilion, fund raising continued, and a planning application was submitted to Winchester City Council. In August 1993 the Foundation for Sport and the Arts gave a grant of £18,500 for a brick built pavilion. Building of phase 1 began shortly afterwards, under the Building sub-Committee of Keith May, Maurice Hibberd, and Cliff Atkinson, and not forgetting the many volunteers who gave their labour. The building project was completed early 1994. In June that year the official opening was performed by Mike Read, Chairman of the Parish Council and Councillor for Winchester & District Council.

Denmead BC official opening by councillor Mike Read.

After the 1996 season several applications for grants were made to the Lottery, Winchester City Council, the Foundation for Sports and Arts, and the Hampshire Playing Fields Association, which resulted in a total of £38,000, being received for the building of an extension to the Pavilion. The prime mover of these applications was Keith May.

The extension was completed for the start of the 1998 season and was officially opened by the Mayor of Winchester on the 18th April 1998. This extension enabled members to play Short Mat Bowling in the winter months, and has proved very popular.

Money is not all one way in the Denmead BC In 1997 £900 was raised for the Rowans Hospice, and in 1998 £1, 100 was raised for the Jubilee Nursery for Children with Special Needs. Both donations were presented at the club's annual dinner.

Denmead BC is a young club with a lot of get up and go, and they deserve all the honours that may befall them. Notably over the past few years they won the 1996 Division 4 league title, and individually in 1995, Glyn Jones won the District Champion of Champions.

1994 Southsea Falcon BC

This club is a combination of various clubs in the history of sides who have played at Southsea since a bowling green was constructed on Southsea Common in the early 1900's. The original team was known as Southsea BC, and in the early days the President was C. Golding. To become a member one had to pay an entrance fee of 2/6d, and an annual subscription of 10/6d, however if you lived off Portsea Island the subscription was reduced to 5/-, presumably this was because you were using public transport to get to the green.

Records do not show when the team changed its name to Southsea Castle, but this was sometime before the Second World War, as the team had many successes with that name and won the Rowland Cup in 1937, 1952, 1954, & 1960. They also won the Mayors Charities Shield in 1947, 1950, 1955, 1957 & 1958. League honours came their way when they won League Division 3 in 1955 and in 1956 before Combination leagues were introduced they won the League Division 2 and League Division 3 titles. In 1959 the club won the League Division 1 title.

There are two Portsmouth & District Presidents attributed to Southsea Castle. In 1937 A.J. Howard held that position and in 1958 E.A. Rogers was in the chair.

In 1934 the National Association of Local Government Officers formed a bowling club, and called it NALGO BC, and played in local inter-departmental competitions between local authorities and hospitals at Southsea. Interest grew to such an extent that the club decided to affiliate to the Portsmouth & District BA and competed in the leagues.

In 1960 the club moved to the Copnor Bridge green and played there for some 10 years. During their time at Copnor Bridge the club won the League Division 3 title in 1963, and were runners up in that league in 1958 & 1961. They also had a member Alan Locke who won the Southsea Open singles title in 1963, and represented Hampshire in the Middleton Cup.

In 1970 the club moved back to Southsea Common, and decided to call themselves Southsea Castle. Later this was to be changed to just Southsea and continued to play under that title until 1993, when the club amalgamated with Falcon BC

Falcon BC was formed in 1963 by a breakaway group of bowlers from Factory Sports. Factory Sports was a social club, which bowled in the Dockyard league and the P&D leagues. The players who formed the nucleus of Falcon BC which included founder members E. Cheater, F. Todd, P. Shulkins, L. Wilson, M. Wood, H. Stanswood, and Percy & Phil Moth, and wanted to play in more competitive games.

Falcon BC became affiliated to the P&D BA and played in the leagues with some success when they won the Rowland Cup in 1973, and winning the Division 2 title in 1972 and the Division 3 title three times in 1964, 1970 & 1993.

The formal amalgamation between Falcon and Southsea took place at the end of 1993, which allowed the new formatted club to play the following year as Southsea Falcon.

In 1996 the club won the Division 3 title.

1996 Emsworth BC

One man, Jack Brown, initially provided the inspiration behind the formation of Emsworth BC. He started the campaign in 1989 with a letter published in the Emsworth Ratepayers Association News, pointing out the lack of bowling facilities in the east of the Havant Borough Council area. In August that year he sought the help of local councillors, and to support his campaign he prepared a detailed paper presenting the case. This paper was put to the Leisure Services Committee in October 1989, and with the help of the local councillors it was agreed, that in principle a bowling facility should be provided in that area, and was included in the Capital Works programme for some future date.

Emsworth BC. Official opening of the green by mayor of Havant with first president Jack Brown.

In 1990 a housing developer wanting to build on a parcel of land to the south of Jubilee Park needed additional land to make the proposal viable. The Council negotiated that in exchange for the additional land, the developer would build a bowling facility.

This did not come to fruition, but in 1993 another developer who wanted to build on the land did a deal with the Council and a bowling facility was now a reality.

During these protracted negotiations a steering group which included Bill Cooper, John Durrant, Alan Lee, Sid Slape, and chaired by Jack Brown, was formed to co-ordinate actions and keep local people aware of the progress.

A public meeting was called in November 1996, which was well supported. Jack Brown was elected as the club's first President, other officers were elected, and the club was officially formed. The President had the honour of bowling the first bowl in May 1997, which was just reward, for this project had taken nearly eight years to bring to fulfilment.

Councillor Alan Emerson the Mayor of Havant officially opened the green on 5th May 1997 and to mark the event a bowling match between all the other Havant Borough clubs was played. A trophy was presented called 'The Emsworth Cup' and this is competed for on an annual basis.

During the first year the club only played friendly matches, but the following year 1998, the club entered the Portsmouth & District leagues, and also played in the local Reflex mixed triples league.

The club has a strong ladies section and in 1999 entered three teams in the ladies P&D leagues.

Emsworth is the youngest club in the district, and as yet the trophy cupboard is bare, but the club does not lack enthusiasm and energy, and look forward to the future with optimism.

The Queens BC, Gosport

The first lawn bowls bowling green in Gosport to be registered was the Queens club and belonged to the Queens Hotel in Sydney Road. The green was situated behind the hotel, and was opened in the early 1900s. The land was sold in 1913 for house building and the club moved along Queens Road, where a new green and pavilion were built. The pavilion is still there to this day and forms part of the Queens Social Club. There is a carved stone in the wall of the club denoting the Officers at that time, among them was Mr J.F. Lee (President), Mr. J.C. Bowers (Secretary) and Mr. J.E. Smith (Captain). Inside the club, there are two large shields mounted on the wall in the billiard room, which were trophies for the Hampshire Bowling Association Competitions. The first being presented by Saxe Weimar BC (Southsea Waverley). And the other one presented by Portsmouth BC. A few years ago they were discovered at

Queens BC: some members on opening day (circa 1900).

the Southsea Waverley Club, refurbished and presented to the Queens Social Club.

In 1935 Mr W. Gay Wright became the President of the Hampshire County Bowling Association and had the honour of receiving the Middleton Cup on the first occasion when the County won the inter County title. He was also President of the P&D in 1928 and 1929.

In 1936 Queens BC gained promotion to Division 1 by winning the Division 2 title and in their first year in the top league became runners up (to Milton Park).

The club continued to operate from this address until the outbreak of World War 2. During preparations for D-Day the area was used by American troops, who used the green as a vehicle park and ruined it. Part of the green area was built on and the rest now forms a car park for the Queens Social Club.

Queens(Gosport)-original clubhouse in background with new extention to the left- the car park used to be the bowling green.

How To Play Bowls

HAVING GOT YOUR ORDERS, IT STILL TAKES THOUGHT — CONCENTRATION —

POISE — CONFIDENCE — SKILL —

SELF-CONTROL AND SOMETHING APPROACHING MOTHER-LOVE, TO BOWL A REALLY SUCCESSFUL WOOD

J.S. Mill – Hampshire county BA President 1956; EBA President 1969.

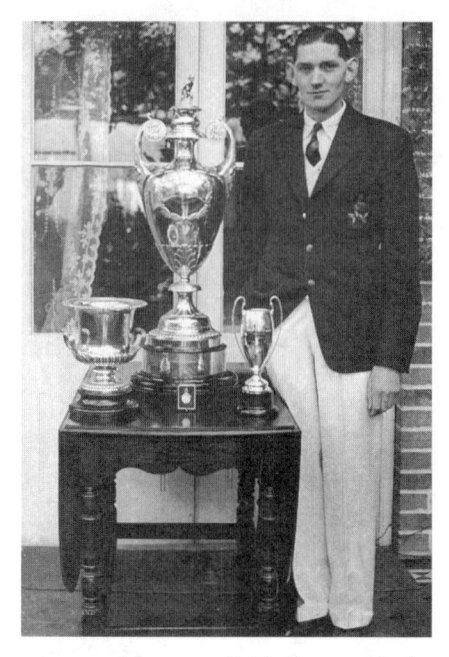

Keith Cross with the EBA National Singles Championship Trophy and the Hampshire Singles Trophy (1938).

Top Fours Competition winners, 1986, Rink skipped by D. Miller, Southsea Waverley.

EBA Presidents

1969   J. S. Mill   Southsea Waverley

International Players

K.I. Cross   Cosham   1937/38/39; 1947/48/49
H. Sawyer   Copnor   1974

EBA National Competitions

Singles Winner
1938   K.I. Cross   Cosham

Fours Winners
1933   B.H. Matthews   )
            H.J. Head   )   Southsea Waverley
            H.W. Johnson   )
            J.W. Rhodes (Skip)   )

Top Fours Competition Winners
1986   Rink Skipped by D. Miller   Southsea Waverley

         D. Dennis (Res.)   Civil Service

1939: C.P. Cross.    **1948:** John C. Glen.    **1952:** W. Christopher.

1960: Capt J. Stout.    **1968:** E.C. Smith.    **1972:** C.F. Hearsey

1976: A.R. Bendall.    **1980:** J.B. North.    **1984:** C.E. Petch.

Hampshire County BA Presidents

1927	J. F. Lee	Gosport
1930	J. E. Rose	College Park
1935	W. Gay Wright	Queens (Gosport)
1939	C. P. Cross, JP	Cosham
1948	Dr. J. C. Glen	Gosport
1952	W. Christopher	Southsea Waverley
1956	J. S. Mill	Southsea Waverley
1960	Capt. J. Stout MM	Portsmouth Co-operative
1964	E. A. Rogers	Southsea Waverley
1968	E. C. Smith	College Park
1972	C. F. Hearsey	Cosham
1976	A. R. Bendall	Southsea Waverley
1980	J. B. North	Alexandra
1984	C. E. Petch	Southsea Waverley
1988	T. H. Bayliss	Fareham
1992	R. H. Edmonds	Hayling Island
1996	R. H. Edmonds	Hayling Island
2000	J. Goble	Alexandra

1988: *T.H. Bayliss.*    **1992 & 1996:** *R.H. Edmonds.*    **2000:** *J. Goble.*

BOWLING DOWN THE YEARS · **99**

County Club Champions 1953 Southsea Waverly.

1948: K.A. Williams. 　**1959:** A. Randal. 　**1983:** W. Charles.

1986: P. Hobday. 　**1990:** D. Bishop. 　**1999:** C. Hayward.

Hampshire County Competitions

County Club Championship
1929	Southsea Waverley
1948	Priory
1953	Southsea Waverley
1956	Copnor
1958	Milton Park
1963	Milton Park
1973	Star & Crescent
1981	Southsea Waverley
1984	Alexandra
1995	Civil Service
1999	Civil Service

Singles Winners
1933	D. Harvey	City of Portsmouth
1936	K. Cross	Cosham
1938	K. Cross	Cosham
1948	K. Williams	Milton Park
1959	A. Randal	Star & Crescent
1983	W. Charles	Alexandra
1986	P. Hobday	Alexandra
1990	D. Bishop	Alexandra
1999	C. Hayward	Civil Service

Under 25 Singles Winners
1999	M. Marchant	Civil Service

1951
J. Stokes &
C. Large.

1958 &
1959
W. John &
F. Neil.

1960
G. Leeson &
E. Akehurst.

1965
I. Williams
& J. Stainer.

1967
R. Lillington
& C. Watts.

1969
R. Nightingale
& F. Cooper.

1972
T. Emerson
& A. Bendall.

1980
E. Brown &
K. Grout.

1984
W. Charles &
A. Ash.

1988
P. Hobday &
D. Bishop.

Hampshire County Competitions *(cont.)*

Pairs Winners

1926	W. Knight & W. Lenton	Southsea Waverley
1933	J. Rhodes & H. Johnson	Southsea Waverley
1934	C. Curtis & E. Phillips	Milton Park
1935	A. Smith & J. Green	Milton Park
1951	J. Stokes & C. Large	Priory
1958	F. Neil & W. John	College Park
1959	F. Neil & W. John	College Park
1960	G. Leeson & E. Akehurst	Civil Service
1963	E. Hill & R. Dickie	Highbury
1965	I. Williams & J. Stainer	Civil Service
1967	C. Watts & R. Lillington	Star & Crescent
1969	R. Nightingale & F. Cooper	Alexandra
1972	A. Bendall & T. Emerson	Southsea Waverley
1980	E. Brown & K. Grout	Star & Crescent
1984	W. Charles & A. Ash	Alexandra
1988	D. Bishop & P. Hobday	Alexandra
1999	C. Gardner & W. Taws	Civil Service

1999
W. Taws & C. Gardener.

1952
Southsea
Waverley
S. Nicholas
A. Hamer
A. Atkey

1957
Milton
Park
F. Forward
K. Cross
S. Wyborn

1959
Southsea
Waverley
R. Parkins
J. Emmerson
G. Russell

1964
Southsea
Waverley
F. Harding
G. Harding
T. Farr

1965
Southern
Electric
(P'mouth)
D. Kewell
R. Gaiger
N. Newell

1976
Rowner
C. Freeman
C. Giles
T. Grant

1983
Star and
Crescent
J. Cox
T. Jamieson
R. Dennison

1987
Alexandra
D. Hall
R. Ward
M. Boltwood

1989
Civil
Service
G. Pratt
K. Newell
P. Smith

1993
Gosport
D. Collins
N. O'Donovan
H. Orr

Hampshire County Competitions *(cont.)*

Triples Winners

1952	Southsea Waverley
1957	Milton Park
1959	Southsea Waverley
1963	Star & Crescent
1964	Southsea Waverley
1965	Southern Electric (Portsmouth)
1976	Rowner
1983	Star & Crescent
1987	Alexandra
1989	Civil Service
1993	Gosport
1996	Civil Service

1996 Civil Service
D Dennis, C. Hayward, N. Brimecombe.

1954 Civil Service:
M. Roberts, H. Cripps, J. Stainer, E. Akehurst.

1964 Milton Park:
D. Moore, R. Scott, E. Holding, D. Grant.

1967 Civil Service
I. Williams, D. Hishon, M. Roberts, J. Stainer.

1971
Alexandra.
A. Wells,
J. Alexander,
L. Hall,
R. Lewis.

1955 & 1956
Milton Park
A. Williams
F. Forward
K. Williams
P. Henley

1966 - Cosham
D. Peddie
H. Morphy
A. Parkhurst
D. Godfrey

1979
Civil Service
D. Dennis
K. Newell
H. Downton
G. Pratt

1982
Alexandra
D. Hall
K. Grout
R. Lillington
W. Charles

Hampshire County Competitions *(cont.)*

Fours Winners

1933	Southsea Waverley
1954	Civil Service
1955	Milton Park
1956	Milton Park
1963	Milton Park
1964	Milton Park
1966	Cosham
1967	Civil Service
1971	Alexandra
1979	Civil Service
1982	Alexandra
1983	Civil Service
1994	I.B.M.

1983 - Civil Service
D. Dennis, K. Newell, H. Downton, G. Pratt

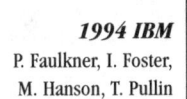

1994 IBM
P. Faulkner, I. Foster, M. Hanson, T. Pullin

1971: *Southsea Waverley*
D. Peddie, F. Shell, A. Bendall

1972: *Gosport*
R. Dear, R. Pearse, J. Newton.

1975: *Copnor*
J. Beveridge, R. Gaiger, S. Wild.

1976: *Alexandra*
C. Reynolds, G. North, W. Drackett.

1979: *Alexandra*
A. Wringe, F. Cooper, J. North.

1980: *Alexandra*
C. Alexander, A. Ash, J. Alexander.

Hampshire County Competitions *(cont.)*

2 Wood Triples Winners *(see opposite page)*
1971	Southsea Waverley
1972	Gosport
1975	Copnor
1976	Alexandra
1979	Alexandra
1980	Alexandra
1999	College Park

Hon. Secretaries Singles Winners
1956	H. Sawyer	Copnor
1959	H. Sawyer	Copnor
1960	H. Sawyer	Copnor
1962	B. Herbert	Forton
1964	G. Day	Milton Casuals
1965	H. Sawyer	Copnor
1966	H. Sawyer	Copnor
1967	P. Butterfield	Cosham
1969	H. Sawyer	Copnor
1971	R. Pearse	Gosport
1973	H. Sawyer	Copnor
1975	H. Sawyer	Copnor
1976	P. Kemp	Bridgemary
1989	R. Cheater	College Park
1995	R. Cheater	College Park
1996	R. Cheater	College Park

R. Cheater, winner 1989, 1995, 1996

BOWLING DOWN THE YEARS · **109**

P&D Presidents 1925 – 1959

1925	Ald. J.F. Lee, JP	Civil Service
1926	J.E. Rose	Alexandra
1927	W.H. Knight	Southsea Waverley
1928	W.G. Wright	Queens Gosport
1929	W.G. Wright	Queens Gosport
1930	W.H. Griffin	Star & Crescent
1931	F.W. Neate	Alexandra
1932	E. Ridsdale	Southsea Waverley
1933	J.G. Hogan	Evening News
1934	C.E. Robinson	Civil Service
1935	J. Williams	City of Portsmouth
1936	J.A. Goodchild	Alexandra
1937	A.J. Coward	Southsea Castle
1938	H. Brewer	City of Portsmouth
1939	J.O. England	Star & Crescent
1940	J.O. England	Star & Crescent
1941	G.F. Smith	Cosham
1942	G.F. Smith	Cosham
1943	H. Brewer	City of Portsmouth
1944	W. Wade	College Park
1945	W. Wade	College Park
1946	E. Allen	Star & Crescent
1947	W. Hooper	Alexandra
1948	W. Christopher	Southsea Waverley
1949	J.H. Ward, M.B.E.	Civil Service
1950	J.S. Mill	Southsea Waverley
1951	A.H. Barron	Pembroke Gardens
1952	Capt. J. Stout, M.M.,	Co-operative
1953	Capt. J. Stout, M.M.,	Co-operative
1954	F. Sellwood	Gosport
1955	J. Moss	College Park
1956	E. Smith	Copnor
1957	G.A. Evans	Alexandra
1958	E.A. Rogers	Southsea Castle
1959	E.S. Hill	Cosham

110 · BOWLING DOWN THE YEARS

P&D Presidents 1960 – 1993

1960	C. E. Petch	Southsea Waverley
1961	G. Leeson	Civil Service
1962	F.C. Street, M.B.E.	Pembroke Gardens
1963	C.F. Hearsey	Cosham
1964	A.V. Organ	Highbury
1965	R. Durkin. B.E.M.	De Havilland
1966	S. Dewey	Milton Casuals
1967	H. Foster	Cosham
1968	J. Lubin	Southsea Waverley
1969	A. Bendall	Southsea Waverley
1970	F. Snelling	Gosport
1971	Dr.J. Hewat	Pembroke Gardens
1972	J.W.T. Sorrell	Star & Crescent
1972	J. Snelling	Star & Crescent
1973	H.J. Moody	Star & Crescent
1974	R.W. Balmer	Priory
1975	J.B. North	Alexandra
1976	J.W. Woolven	Waterlooville
1977	A.A. Haigh	Highbury
1978	E. Facey	Priory
1979	G. Looseley	Southsea Waverley
1980	J.R. Barron	Pembroke Gardens
1981	W. Giles	Moneyfield
1982	A. Gundry	Waterlooville
1983	J. Whitehill	Southsea Waverley
1984	A. Bowen	Highbury
1985	C. Thompson	Alexandra
1986	R. Edmonds	Star & Crescent
1987	R. Cooper	Highbury
1988	Capt. D. Bateman	Star & Crescent
1989	N.S. Townsend	Gosport
1990	G. Meaden	Purbrook
1991	R. Standley	Alexandra
1992	D. Wildman	I. B. M.
1993	T. Stone-Houghton	Portsmouth Water Co.

P&D Presidents 1994 – 2000

1994	W. Hellier	Cowplain
1995	W. Lamb	Cosham
1996	I. Robb	Highbury
1997	B. Luff	Cosham
1998	S. Sprake	Star & Crescent
1999	B. Ivemey	City of Portsmouth
2000	J. Powell	Waterlooville

Keith Cross

One of Portsmouth's more famous bowlers is Keith Cross, who in 1938 became the EBA National Singles Champion at the age of 27, extremely young for bowlers in those days.

Keith first played seriously at the age of 21 in 1932 and although he lived in Drayton, travelled to the Isle of Wight each Saturday to play bowls for Ryde. In 1936 he got his first representative game for Hampshire against Middlesex, played at Southsea. In 1937 he played for England in the International series at Llandrindod Wells; in 1938 at Larne N. Ireland and in 1939 at Lensbury BC at Teddington, Middlesex.

After the war, Keith was recalled to the England team and in 1947 played at number 3 to G. Wright at Newport, S. Wales. In 1948 the series was played at Bangor, N. Ireland and Keith recalls that the wind was coming from the north, the coldest conditions he has experienced on a bowling green.

In 1949 Keith played skip at Preston Park Brighton. The organisers' had decided to put screens up around the greens and wanted to charge spectators 2/6d to enter. Needless to say there were very few people willing to pay; they preferred to watch local sides playing on adjacent greens. On one end during this match he found himself eight down with one wood in his hand. He could only play one hand as the other hand was blocked; that hand happened to be a very tricky side, but had to be played. He put it out wide and the wood came into the head at right angles and ended up alongside the jack!

Unfortunately, his international career came to an end due to illness. When better he had further trials but was unsuccessful in regaining his place.

Keith and his father (who was the Hampshire County President from 1939 to 1944) were founder members of the Cosham BC. Keith played there until 1950, at which time he transferred to Milton Park BC. Keith was President twice and Secretary at Milton Park.

In December 1935, Keith and his father, who were also members of Wellington BC (N.Z.) were entered by the club in the singles, pairs & fours of the Dominion Tournament in New Zealand. He stayed until April 1936, a visit he was to repeat again from November 1938 to March 1939, and it was while he was playing there that he first came across the 'firing

Keith Cross and his father Conyngham P. Cross with some of their bowling trophies in 1938.

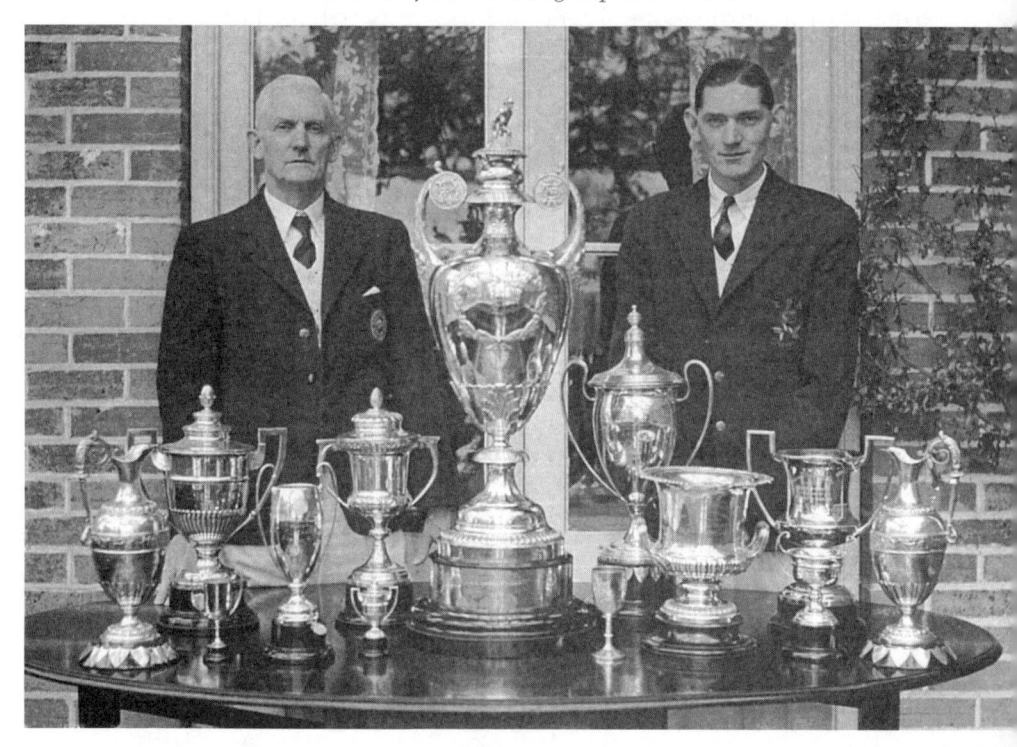

shot'. On his return to Portsmouth in 1938, whilst playing for Cosham against City of Portsmouth, he applied his newly learnt skill and was promptly booed by the spectators around the green! At the end of the game the opposing players refused to shake hands. The firing shot was 'not the done thing' before 1960, until David Bryant made it acceptable.

Keith was Hampshire County Singles Champion in 1936 & 1938. In 1957, with F. Forward & S. Wyborne he won the County Triples title. In 1963 F. Forward, F. Moore, G. Hunt and Keith (as skipper) won the County Fours title.

Keith played 83 times in the Middleton Cup and was in the winning teams of 1963, 1967 and 1968. In 1967 against Middlesex Keith skipped an all Portsmouth rink of H. Sawyer (Copnor), A. Hamer (Southsea Waverley), J. Stainer (Civil Service) and was a winning rink.

Keith played bowls up to his retirement from the game in 1988, some 56 years, and in all that time he used the same bowls, the largest lignum bowl you could get ($5\tfrac{3}{16}$ inches).

Upon his retirement from the game Keith busied himself in his garden and supplied the Sweet Peas as floral decoration for the tables at the County Presidents Day, and to quote his words, *"Grown for pleasure, to give pleasure"*. (1970)

League Championships

The following represents league tables based on the number of times a club has won the relevant league, and been runners up in that league over the years it has been competed for.

    For winning   5 points awarded
    Runners up   1 point awarded

League Division 1

	Won	*R/U*	*Points*
Milton Park	22	3	113
Southsea Waverley	10	16	66
Portsmouth Civil Service	10	8	58
Alexandra	10	5	55
Star & Crescent	8	1	41
College Park	3	7	22
I. B. M.	2	2	12
Cosham	1	6	11
City of Portsmouth	2	-	10
Copnor	1	4	9
Priory	1	1	6
Portsmouth North	1	-	5
Southsea Castle	1	-	5
Leigh Park	-	2	2
Gosport	-	1	1
Moneyfield	-	1	1
Queens (Gosport)	-	1	1

League Division 2

	Won	*R/U*	*Points*
Milton Park	7	5	40
College Park	7	2	37
Gosport	6	6	36
Priory	5	8	33
Pembroke Gardens	4	10	30
Copnor	4	3	23
Star & Crescent	4	3	23
City of Portsmouth	3	4	19
Alexandra	3	2	17
Waterlooville	3	2	17
Cosham	3	-	15
Leigh Park	3	-	15
Rowner	2	1	11
Highbury	1	3	8
Milton Casuals	1	2	7
Falcon	1	1	6
Portsmouth Civil Service	1	1	6
Southsea Castle	1	1	6
Clarence	1	-	5
Hayling Island	1	-	5
I. B. M.	1	-	5
Queens (Gosport)	1	-	5
S. E. S. A.	1	-	5
Southsea Waverley	1	-	5
Portsmouth Water Co.	-	3	3
Vospers	-	2	2
Airspeed	-	1	1
Factory Sports	-	1	1
Fareham	-	1	1

League Division 3

	Won	R/U	Points
Co-operative	4	2	22
Fareham	4	2	22
Gas Undertaking	3	4	19
Cosham	3	3	18
Forton	3	3	18
Highbury	3	1	16
Vospers	3	1	16
Falcon	3	-	15
Bridgemary	2	2	12
College Park	2	1	11
Rowner	2	1	11
Post Office	2	-	10
Southsea Castle	2	-	10
Lee on the Solent	2	-	10
Naismith	1	4	9
Passenger Transport	1	3	8
NALGO	1	2	7
Waterlooville	1	2	7
Airspeed	1	1	6
City of Portsmouth	1	1	6
Leigh Park	1	1	6
Purbrook Heath	1	1	6
SESA	1	1	6
Factory Sports	1	-	5
I. B. M.	1	-	5
Milton Casuals	1	-	5
Portsmouth Water Co.	1	-	5
Priory	1	-	5
Southsea Falcon	1	-	5
Alexandra	-	4	4
Copnor	-	3	3
Hayling Island	-	3	3
Portsmouth Civil Service and Joiners Sports			2

Cowplain, De Havilland, Gosport, Southsea Waverley, and Welburns all have 1 point.

League Division 4

	Won	*R/U*	*Points*
Bedhampton	3	2	17
Bridgemary	2	1	11
Highbury	1	1	6
Lee on the Solent	1	1	6
City of Portsmouth	1	-	5
Cowplain	1	-	5
Crofton	1	-	5
Denmead	1	-	5
Forton	1	-	5
Hayling Island	1	-	5
Portsmouth Post Office	1	-	5
Eastney	-	2	2

Co-operative, Drayton, Lakeside, Passenger Transport, Portchester, and Purbrook Heath have 1 point

League Champions

Division 1 • League Champions

Winners receive a cup presented by Col.J.W. Peters
Runners up receive a cup presented by N.F. Dutson

1925	Southsea Waverley
1926	Southsea Waverley
1927	City of Portsmouth
1928	Southsea Waverley
1929	Southsea Waverley
1930	Milton Park
1931	City of Portsmouth
1932	Milton Park
1933	Milton Park
1934	Milton Park
1935	Milton Park
1936	Milton Park
1937	Milton Park
1938	Milton Park
1939	Milton Park
1940	No competition
1941	No competition
1942	Copnor
1943	Portsmouth North
1944	College Park
1945	Alexandra
1946	Unknown
1947	Milton Park
1948	Milton Park
1949	Civil Service

1950	Milton Park
1951	Priory
1952	Milton Park
1953	College Park
1954	Milton Park
1955	Southsea Waverley
1956	Milton Park
1957	Milton Park
1958	Milton Park
1959	Southsea Castle
1960	Cosham
1961	Milton Park
1962	Milton Park
1963	Milton Park
1964	Milton Park
1965	Milton Park
1966	Civil Service
1967	Star & Crescent
1968	Star & Crescent
1969	Southsea Waverley
1970	Star & Crescent
1971	Alexandra
1972	Alexandra
1973	Star & Crescent
1974	Star & Crescent
1975	Star & Crescent
1976	Civil Service
1977	Alexandra
1978	Alexandra
1979	Star & Crescent
1980	Civil Service
1981	Star & Crescent
1982	Southsea Waverley

1983	Alexandra
1984	Alexandra
1985	Alexandra
1986	Southsea Waverley
1987	Alexandra
1988	Alexandra
1989	Civil Service
1990	Civil Service
1991	IBM
1992	Southsea Waverley
1993	Civil Service
1994	College Park
1995	IBM
1996	Civil Service
1997	Civil Service
1998	Southsea Waverley
1999	Civil Service

Division 2 • League Champions

Winners receive a cup presented by J.E. Rose
Runners up receive a cup presented by W.G. Wright

1927	Alexandra
1928	Milton Park
1929	Southsea Waverley
1930	Alexandra
1931	Clarence
1932	Milton Park
1933	College Park
1934	Gosport
1935	Pembroke Gardens
1936	Queens
1937	Cosham
1938	Star & Crescent
1939-1946	No competition
1947	Priory
1948	Alexandra
1949	Milton Park
1950	College Park
1951	City of Portsmouth
1952	Cosham
1953	Star & Crescent
1954	City of Portsmouth
1955	College Park
1956	Southsea Castle
1957	Priory
1958	Cosham
1959	College Park
1960	Highbury
1961	Civil Service
1962	Priory
1963	Milton Casuals
1964	Gosport

1965	Copnor
1966	Priory
1967	Gosport
1968	S.E.S.A.
1969	Pembroke Gardens
1970	Milton Park
1971	Priory
1972	Falcon
1973	College Park
1974	Pembroke Gardens
1975	Milton Park
1976	City of Portsmouth
1977	Rowner
1978	Copnor
1979	College Park
1980	Milton Park
1981	Leigh Park
1982	Milton Park
1983	Copnor
1984	Pembroke Gardens
1985	Leigh Park
1986	Waterlooville
1987	IBM
1988	Gosport
1989	Waterlooville
1990	Gosport
1991	Rowner
1992	Copnor
1993	Leigh Park
1994	Star & Crescent
1995	Hayling Island
1996	Star & Crescent
1997	College Park
1998	Waterlooville
1999	Gosport

Division 3 • League Champions

Winners receive a cup presented by J.F. Hooper
Runners up receive a cup presented by Lt.Cdr. W.G. Bishop

1933	Unknown
1934	Unknown
1935	College Park
1936	Cosham
1937	Unknown
1938	Unknown
1939	Unknown
1947	Unknown
1948	Unknown
1949	College Park
1950	Airspeed
1951	Passenger Transport
1952	Forton
1953	Highbury
1954	Priory
1955	Southsea Castle
1956	Southsea Castle
1957	Cosham
1958	Milton Casuals
1959	Factory Sports
1960	Co-operative
1961	Gas Undertaking
1962	Co-operative
1963	N.A.L.G.O.
1964	Falcon
1965	Forton
1966	Waterlooville
1967	S.E.S.A.
1968	Highbury

1969	Gas Undertaking
1970	Falcon
1971	Rowner
1972	Gas Undertaking
1973	Bridgemary
1974	City of Portsmouth
1975	Naismith
1976	Highbury
1977	Leigh Park
1978	Vospers
1979	Bridgemary
1980	Co-operative
1981	Fareham
1982	IBM
1983	Fareham
1984	Water Company
1985	Co-operative
1986	Rowner
1987	Fareham
1988	Vospers
1989	Post Office
1990	Cosham
1991	Vospers
1992	Fareham
1993	Falcon
1994	Lee on the Solent
1995	Forton
1996	Southsea Falcon
1997	Purbrook Heath
1998	Lee on the Solent
1999	Post Office

Division 4 • League Champions

Winners receive a cup presented by C. Thompson
Runners up receive a cup presented by R. Cooper

1986	Lee on the Solent
1987	Crofton
1988	Post Office
1989	Bedhampton
1990	Hayling Island
1991	Bridgemary
1992	Forton
1993	Cowplain
1994	City of Portsmouth
1995	Bedhampton
1996	Denmead
1997	Highbury
1998	Bridgemary
1999	Bedhampton

Trophies for Combination Leagues

Combination 1	Winners cup presented by A. Wringe
	Runners up cup presented by E. C. Smith
Combination 2	Winners cup presented by C. E. Petch
	Runners up cup presented by A. Bendall
Combination 3	Winners cup presented by A. A. Haigh
	Runners up cup presented by Unknown
Combination 4	Winners shield presented by R. Edmonds
	Runners up bowl presented by G. Pook
Combination 5	Winners shield presented by G. Meadon
	Runners up shield presented by C. May
Combination 6	Winners cup presented by R. Edmonds
	Runners up shield presented by G. Hannah
MW Triples Town	Winners cup presented by W. Hellier
	Runners up cup presented by L. Jones
MW Triples Dist.	Winners cup presented by W. Hellier
	Runners up cup presented by L. Jones

Trophies for Competitions

Champion of Champions	
Winner	J. Mill trophy presented by A. R. Bendall
Runner up	Cup presented by J. Whitehall
Singles	
Winner	Cup presented by H. Filer
Runner up	Cup presented by J. Lubin
Over 60's Singles	
Winner	G. Leeson Cup presented by Portsmouth Civil Service
Under 25's Singles	
Winner	Shield presented by Canada Life
Pairs	
Winners	Cup presented by A. F. Warrilow
Triples	
Winners	Cup presented by Ald. F. Miles CBE.
Fours	
Winners	Rose Bowl presented by J. Smith

128 · BOWLING DOWN THE YEARS

The Leagues: Past, Present and Future

The first league started in 1925, and there were obviously only a few local clubs competing initially. Records being a bit hazy we can only deduce that the league consisted of about ten clubs namely Southsea Waverley, City of Portsmouth, Southsea, Queens (Gosport), Star & Crescent, Alexandra, Copnor, Civil Service, Milton Park, and Pembroke Gardens.

The first winners were Southsea Waverley who were awarded The Peters Bowl, which was presented by Colonel J. W. Peters.

A second division was formed in 1927, followed by a third division in 1933.

With World War 2 intervening, it was not until a few years after cessation of hostilities that the popularity started to gain momentum.

The first Combination league was started in 1956 to cater for the increase in the sports popularity, and was soon followed by other Combination leagues. A Fourth division proper was started in 1986.

Currently the Portsmouth & District run twelve leagues including the mid-week triples, which theoretically takes in 1, 500 bowlers, playing in roughly 66 games per week.

Until a few years ago all results were entered and calculated manually, which probably was not too bad in the early days but as the leagues have increased in size, it became quite a burdensome job. Having being personally instrumental in introducing computers to Victory I. BC some ten years ago for administration and league records, when I was asked to take over the P&D League Secretary's job, I immediately had a custom built program written for all P&D League records.

Results and league tables are forwarded to the News weekly using E-mail. One club is already using E-mail to report the result of their matches. There is no reason why this method cannot be extended, as more and more people become computer literate.

Who knows what the future holds for us? If all clubs were connected to the Internet it would be possible, even now, to publish all results and league tables on a Web site so that they were readily available and right up to date.

The rapid growth of Indoor Bowls facilities in this area, combined with unreliable and sometimes unpleasant weather, makes players (particularly the older ones) reluctant to commit themselves, especially early in the season, to outdoor League bowls on cold, wet and windy evenings. To some extent this has been offset by the advent of the afternoon midweek Triples League. I think therefore that there will be some reduction in interest in the evening Leagues, and more interest in midweek afternoon Leagues, and Indoor Summer Leagues.

In the fairly recent past there has been a considerable growth in Mixed Bowls. This trend is, I believe likely to continue firstly because Bowls is about the only sport where men and women can compete on virtually equal terms and secondly because of the political climate and consequent financial pressures. (e. g. grants and rebates being denied if there is any form of discrimination).

Richard Edmonds

The Gwyn Guy Trophy

In the course of conversation at a Portsmouth dinner, the keen friendly rivalry between Portsmouth & District and Southampton & District was raised, which prompted a discussion as to who was the stronger of the Districts in Hampshire. There was a tentative offer by Portsmouth to provide a trophy for inter- divisional matches. On the 7th May 1963 Mr. Guy reported the general banter to a Southampton Committee meeting. The Southampton Secretary was instructed to contact not only Portsmouth, but also Bournemouth & District and Aldershot & District to arrange a meeting and formulate the rules and any other details that may be required.

On the 8th May 1964, again at a Southampton Committee meeting the question was raised as to the outcome of the various letters written to the other Associations, and what arrangements had been made regarding the trophy. As no trophy was forthcoming from other sources, the Southampton

Steve Sprake, president of P&D receiving the trophy in 1998 from Gwyn Guy.

Committee agreed to put up a trophy, at which point Mr. Gwyn Guy kindly offered to donate a suitable trophy. This offer was gratefully accepted with unanimous approval and that it be known as "The Gwyn Guy Trophy"

At a meeting on the 9th November 1964, held at the Atherley BC between the four District Secretaries, it was agreed that the competition be known as The Gwyn Guy Trophy, and that it would be competed for annually commencing in 1965. The basis of play to be a standard match of 21 ends over 6 rinks at an agreed venue with 2 points awarded to the winning team, with points shared in the event of a tie. In all matches one extra end to be played.

The first competition took place at various venues around the County districts, and resulted in a win for Bournemouth with Portsmouth in the runners up spot.

This format continued until 1968 at which time the matches were played on adjacent greens at one location over successive weekends.

The competition has flourished over the years under the guidance and hard work put in by the Competition Secretary, assisted by the support of the various Associations. In the year 2000 Brian Brouard, who has been the Secretary for the past 15 years will be standing down.

The present competition is played between Aldershot, Basingstoke, Portsmouth and Southampton & District Bowling Associations, and the keen friendly rivalry continues to this day.

Aldershot has won 3 times
Basingstoke has won twice
Bournemouth has won twice
Portsmouth has won 13 times
Southampton has won 15 times

The Rowland Cup

The Rowland Cup was donated by Sir John Rowland to the Portsmouth & District Bowling Association in 1928. It was to be competed for between clubs in the district, and all proceeds were to go to the Amenities and Comforts Fund for Hospital Nursing Staff, at the Royal Hospital Portsmouth.

The Rowland Cup • Winners

1928	Pembroke Gardens
1929	Milton Park
1930	Gosport
1931	East Anglian
1932	City of Portsmouth
1933	Pembroke Gardens.
1934	Alexandra
1935	Southsea Waverley
1936	Copnor
1937	Southsea Castle
1938	Priory
1939-42	No competition
1943	College Park
1944	College Park
1945	Civil Service
1946	Copnor
1947	Southsea Waverley
1948	City of Portsmouth
1949	Airspeed
1950	Priory
1951	Milton Park
1952	Southsea Castle
1953	College Park

1954	Southsea Castle
1955	Southsea Waverley
1956	Milton Park
1957	Southsea Waverley
1958	Southsea Waverley
1959	City of Portsmouth
1960	Southsea Castle
1961	Milton Park
1962	Civil Service
1963	College Park
1964	College Park
1965	Milton Casuals
1966	Civil Service
1967	Copnor
1968	Civil Service
1969	Alexandra
1970	Southsea Waverley
1971	Southsea Waverley
1972	Southsea Waverley
1973	Falcon
1974	College Park
1975	Copnor
1976	Civil Service
1977	Civil Service
1978	Civil Service
1979	Civil Service
1980	Star & Crescent
1981	Alexandra
1982	Southsea Waverley
1983	Civil Service
1984	Southsea Waverley
1985	Southsea Waverley
1986	Leigh Park

1987	Civil Service
1988	Alexandra
1989	Alexandra
1990	IBM
1991	Civil Service
1992	IBM
1993	Southsea Waverley
1994	Alexandra
1995	Rowner
1996	Civil Service
1997	Gosport
1998	Star & Crescent
1999	IBM

A trophy was donated in 1999 by R. Edmonds for the runners up in this competition. It is known as the Haslar Hospital Cup, and is in keeping with the original concept of this competition that proceeds should go to a hospital charity.

The first recipient of the Haslar Cup was Gosport.

The Mayors Charities Bowling Shield

This was an annual inter club trophy, which was presented to the Portsmouth & District B. A. in 1928 by the Southsea Waverley BC This trophy can been seen on display in the billiard and snooker hall at the Southsea Waverley club.

1928	Pembroke Gardens
1929	Southsea Waverley
1930	Milton Park
1931	Pembroke Gardens
1932	Alexandra
1933	Star & Crescent
1934	Star & Crescent
1935	Southsea Waverley
1936	Star & Crescent
1937	Copnor
1938	Milton Park
1939	Cosham
1940	Priory
1943	Civil Service
1947	Southsea Castle
1948	Priory
1949	Forton
1950	Southsea Castle
1951	City of Portsmouth
1952	Copnor
1953	De Havilland
1954	Star & Crescent
1955	Southsea Castle
1956	Star & Crescent
1957	Southsea Castle
1958	Southsea Castle
1959	Southsea Waverley

The Southsea Open Tournament

The first Southsea Open was staged in 1928, just 3 years after the formation of the Portsmouth & District Bowling Association. It was run by the P&DBA on behalf of the Portsmouth City Council, the object of which was to encourage visitors to the City. In the early advertisements Southsea was described as 'Facing Spithead and the Isle of Wight'.

In the early years the tournament was known as the Southsea Amateur Open Bowls Tournament, and was held during the third week in July, and the entrance fee allowed free admission to South Parade Pier for the competitor and one friend during the bowling week

An official Hotel and Entertainment Guide was available for purchase at 9d. in an effort to encourage families to visit the City. It was stated in advertisements that 'One week at Southsea is worth two weeks elsewhere, so spend a happy holiday at Southsea Open Bowls Tournament'.

In the beginning the value of the prizes amounted to £250. and remained at that figure until 1950 when it was increased to £320. The advertising dropped the word 'Amateur' in 1957, when the prize money was increased to £500.

On the 50th anniversary of the Tournament in 1985 the prize money reached £1,000.

In 1959 it was stated that this was an 'Open Bowls Tournament held on good greens and in good company' This was eventually dropped in 1983.

In 1965 it was decided to change the date of the competition to the first full week in August, where it has remained to date.

The Tournament has been run every year since 1928, with the exception of the War years 1940-1946, and throughout its history has maintained most of the original concepts and principles in trying to generate visitors to Portsmouth. With this in mind, a visitors only mixed pairs competition is run on the Sunday prior to the main competitions, which start on Monday.

For many years this was the only Tournament on the South Coast that run Ladies and Gents competitions on the same week.

Bowling Greens

Many changes have taken place over the years, and recently we have seen the introduction from imperial measurements to metrication, but the game of bowls is initially one of drawing to the jack. This is only possible if the running surface is maintained to a reasonably high standard.

Growing grass for bowls greens and golf courses requires time, knowledge and experience. There are no short cuts. Currently the average material costs excluding labour, to maintain a bowling green to an acceptable standard is £1,000 per annum.

In an ideal world, every bowls club would employ a full time qualified Greenkeeper. For obvious reasons this is not always practical and alternative arrangements are necessary. This could be a club member, a private contractor or the local council.

The willing club member is often the subject of criticism by his fellow members. The private contractor and local councils have workloads, which require each job to be completed within the time allowed and with the minimum thought and attention. For one reason or another the work programme is not always carried out in the correct order and as a result the green deteriorates and the players complain. It can take up to 4 years to recover a deteriorated green, which involves a lot of additional hard work, with the associated extra costings.

The answer to the problem is not easy to establish.

- To increase the fees would not go down well with the majority of members but such a change would allow an expert to be employed.

- How about an artificial green with the minimum of maintenance? The material is expensive and has a limited life, however the cost is a known fact and can be amortized over the period of its life span.

Assuming that we accept artificial surfaces one train of thought suggests that we play indoors all the year. No sun, no wind, no rain. Surely this is not the answer.

The installation of an outdoor artificial green costs close to £75,000 + VAT. This does not include the cost of the land. Annual maintenance costs approximately £400. The life expectancy of the carpet is at least 10 years, and with the cost of the carpet and underlay at around £28,000 would mean an budget of approximately £3,200 per annum.

In conclusion, I should like to tell of a true experience of mine. During the sixties, I was with a major canned food manufacturer in North West London. The company employed a full time Greenkeeper for the staff's bowling green. The green was reputed to be one of the best in Middlesex.

The Greenkeeper retired and was not replaced and the care of the green became a series of job cards in the maintenance department. At one period, the green was so badly burnt by fertiliser that the green had to be watered continuously for two weeks.

There is another episode, the truth of which I cannot vouch for. The job cards became out of order, the green was fertilised one day and then cut the next day. The mower operator took some of the cuttings home and had the finest lawn in his neighbourhood!

Len Janes
EBA Greens Maintenance Advisory Scheme
Hampshire County Representative.

The Future

It is important that as bowlers we encourage the younger generation to take up the game of bowls. The photographs below show that the game can be enjoyed and very rewarding to all those who participate.

With this in mind the Portsmouth & District Bowling Association run an annual knockout competition for the under 25's, with prizes given down to the losing semi-finalists.

Previous winners of this competition are:

1997 Alex Marchant (Alexandra)
1998 Alex Vernal (Cowplain)
1999 Steve Robertson (IBM)

Matthew Marchant
England U-25 Indoor International, Hampshire County BA U-25 Singles Champion.

Steve Robertson
England U-25 Indoor International

Club Names from The Past

Queens BC (Gosport) 1900 – 1939
Played at Queens Hotel, Sydney Road, & Queens Road

Southsea BC 1900 – 1928   *Played at Southsea Common*

Factory Sports MED (Managers Engineering Dept.) 1921-74
Played at Southsea Common & Alexandra Park

Evening News Sports 1926 – 1939   *Played at Southsea Common*

Clarence BC 1927 – 1938   *Played at Pembroke Gardens*

Southsea Castle BC 1928 – 1970   *Played at Southsea Castle*

NALGO 1934 – 1989   *Played at Milton Park, Southsea Common, & Copnor*

Portsmouth North BC 1941–1955
Played at College Park & Alexandra Park

Ophir BC 1945 – 1963   *Played at Alexandra Park*

Portsmouth City Police 1946 – 1952   *Played at Milton Park*

De-Havilland (Hawker Siddeley, Moneyfields) 1948-88
Played at Southsea Castle, Moneyfields, & Cosham

Milton Casuals 1949 – 1973   *Played at Milton Park & Canoe Lake*

Southern Electric Service Assc. 1951 – 1973 *Played at Cosham*

Joiner Sports & Social Club 1959 – 1972
Played at Southsea Castle & Alexandra Park

De la Rue 1981 – 1986 *Played at Drayton Park*

Saxe-Weimar (1896) Southsea Waverley

East Anglians (1926) Priory

PIMCO Managers (1935) Co-operative

Portsmouth Passenger Transport(1947) Eastney

DECSA (1948) – Welburns (1971) Lakeside

Portsmouth Gas Undertaking (1948) Gas Social

Falcon (1963) Southsea Falcon

C.J.C. Drayton (1963) Naismith

Airspeed

Craneswater

Metal Box

Acknowledgements

Councillor David Horne JP

The Right Worshipful the Lord Mayor of the City of Portsmouth

Portsmouth City Museum and Records Office

Portsmouth City Libraries

Gosport Borough Council

Havant Museum

Havant Borough Libraries

English Bowling Association

Hampshire County Bowling Association

Keith Cross

Dave Dennis

Richard Edmonds

Brian Brouard

Len Janes

N. (Dick) Brimicombe

The Rose Studio (Photographers)

All the clubs who kindly contributed 'potted histories' and other relevant information.

Commandments of Bowling

"Thou shalt not put any game before Bowls"

"Thou shalt not take unto thee any golf club, tennis racket or any idol of mind or body that would alienate thee from the one and only game."

"Thou shalt not speak lightly of thy Skip, nor ever think of him without due reverence."

"Honour thy President, thy Secretary and thy Selectors, that thy place may long be secure in the contests of thy club against all comers."